What the Readers Say

"The Man in the Scarlet Robe is a fascinating journey into the issues that stir debate in the 20th century world of Christian scholarship. The authors have succeeded in being... both readable and easily understood. This book is a first rate analysis of the movements in the contemporary history of Christian thought. It belongs in the library of every serious modern Christian."

The Rt. Rev. John Shelby Spong
Author of *Resurrection: Myth or Reality?*

"As Jesus is stripped of his scarlet robe, so too will readers find former assumptions, language, images and convictions about Jesus uncovered as they follow the story of the past and present search for the historical Jesus. This book actually invites us to go beyond the quest of scholarship by embarking on our own quest for the man who has made headlines for thousands of years."

The Rev. Dr. M. Jean Stairs
Queen's Theological College

"The Man in the Scarlet Robe is as gripping as a P.D. James detective novel. I couldn't put it down until I had finished it. ...a good read and a good survey of the search for Jesus."

Rev. Dr. Graham Scott
Editor, *Theological Digest & Outlook*

"An engaging and lively romp through the minefield of Jesus research. The authors lead their readers on a merry chase along the main routes — and some of the byways — of discussion about the historical Jesus. It is a sure-footed walk through no-man's land, calculated to introduce the players and the issues, without taking sides."

Professor Peter Richardson
University of Toronto

"The Man in the Scarlet Robe brilliantly draws together in one easy-to-read book the known facts, the suppositions, the possibilities and even the bizarre theories of a diverse body of scripture detectives. A must-read for believer and skeptic."

Roy Bonisteel
Author, Broadcaster

The Man in the Scarlet Robe:
Two Thousand Years of Searching for Jesus

Canadian Cataloguing in Publication Data

McAteer, Michael R., 1933-
    The man in the scarlet robe : two thousand years
    of searching for Jesus

Includes bibliographical references.
ISBN 1-55134-042-9

1. Jesus Christ - Historicity. I. Steinhauser, Michael G.
II Title.

BT303.2.M33 1996   232.9'08   C96-930212-6

The United Church Publishing House
3250 Bloor St. West, 4th floor
Etobicoke, Ontario, Canada
M8X 2Y4

Acquisition: Catherine Wilson
Development: Peter Gordon White
Editing: Elizabeth Phinney
Design: Gordon Szendrey

♻ 960006

Printed in Canada

THE MAN
IN THE SCARLET ROBE

Two Thousand Years
of Searching for Jesus

Michael R. McAteer • Michael G. Steinhauser

THE UNITED CHURCH
PUBLISHING HOUSE

Contents

Preface

The Roman soldiers stripped the young Galilean Jew and placed a scarlet robe upon him. They put a crown of thorns on his head, a reed in his right hand, and knelt before him, mocking him, saying, "Hail, King of the Jews!" Then they stripped him of the robe, put his own clothes back on him, and led him away to crucify him (Matt. 27:27-31).

After a hiatus of several decades, scholarly research into the man in the scarlet robe, known to history as Jesus of Nazareth, is undergoing a dramatic revival. And starting about fifteen years ago, this renewed interest has spread outside the walls of academia and church institutions. Television documentaries reconstruct the life and times of Jesus; movies present him in contemporary settings; and best-seller lists include "Jesus" books by biblical scholars. Secular writers, some propounding bizarre theories about his life and death, add spice to the public appetite for details about a man who died almost two thousand years ago.

Noted clerics fuel the fires of theological debate by questioning the basic tenets of Christianity, and a small group of biblical scholars, known as the Jesus Seminar, challenge traditional images of Jesus. Each new theory rekindles the flames of controversy.

There are said to be more than 70,000 known biographies of the man known as Jesus Christ—Jesus, the Greek form of the Hebrew *Joshua*, and Christ from the Greek *Christos*, the anointed one. But "biography" may be a misnomer, given the paucity of information free of theological overlay. There are no eye-witness accounts of

Jesus' life. There were no investigative reporters, no tape recorders, no video cameras around to record his words and deeds for posterity. There is no evidence that he wrote anything. The little we do know about him was written by others.

So what can we know with certainty about Jesus? Where does the information we do have come from? How much is based on historical fact? How much comes to us filtered through a believing church?

Historians tell us that Jesus preached at a time when there was no shortage of messiahs, wonder-workers, and prophets. Why then did Jesus and his message live on in the annals of history while the dreams of other prophets and charismatics were dispersed like desert sand? Was it all part of a divine plan, a revelation, as many devout Christians believe? Or was it all due to a series of fortuitous events? The dreams of one charismatic called the Teacher of Righteousness were lost until an Arab shepherd boy found the Dead Sea Scrolls in a Judean cave in 1947; the dreams of another charismatic named Jesus were preserved by a believing community and, in time, shaped the destiny of Western culture.[1]

Jesus has been called one of the great question marks of all history. People tried to figure him out while he was alive and we continue to do so today. Some have resolved the riddle to their own satisfaction. For others, Jesus remains a mysterious figure obscured by the mists of time. What did he look like? Was he real or imaginary or a little of both, as is the case with all historic figures? Was he, as many claim, both fully human and fully divine? Or was he simply a mortal being like the rest of us? One question leads to another.

Perhaps the biggest question—the greatest mystery—is why, in this high-tech secular age, when humans are probing the very heavens and unlocking the secrets of the DNA, do people continue to discuss, talk about, even argue about, a man who died a shameful death on a Roman cross so long ago? Just what is there about "this peasant that galvanizes people to find him special—special to their lives?"[2] Why does a sceptical, non-Christian film director spend more than ten years researching the historical Jesus with the hope of producing a "true" picture of Jesus the man, free from the excrescence of church and history?[3]

Matthew's Gospel tells us that at approximately three o'clock on Good Friday, Jesus cried out in a loud voice, "My God, my God, why have you forsaken me?" and then breathed his last (Matt. 27:46-50). His closest followers scattered, terrified by what had happened. By all the "laws of historical logic,"[4] that should have ended the story. Jesus should never have been heard from again. Instead, the man who was forced by mocking Roman soldiers to don a scarlet robe before they crucified him inspired a religious movement whose followers have spread the Christian message to the far corners of the globe.

Introduction

The seeds of this book were sown at a 1984 visit to an Anglican church, just north of Toronto, where a "portrait" of Jesus was on display. At the time, I was religion editor of *The Toronto Star*, Canada's largest circulation daily newspaper. As well as covering religion on a daily basis, I was also responsible for writing a weekend article for the paper's religion page. The intriguing claim by English-born portrait artist Chris Hooper, that he had painted a true portrait of Jesus, promised to be the basis for an interesting weekend feature.

The portrait was that of a full-bearded man in his thirties. Thick, auburn hair, parted in the middle, hung to his shoulders and framed a swarthy face. The hazel eyes were gentle and frank. In contrast, there was a toughness, a sense of disillusionment, to the set of the lips that belied the eyes' trusting nature.

This, Hooper told me, was no less than the definitive portrait of Jesus Christ. Based on seven years of painstaking research, and blending artistic creativity with the techniques of modern science, this twentieth-century artist had produced what he claimed was the most accurate depiction ever of the man who had died almost two thousand years ago. Considering the variety and scope of artistic images of Jesus that have come down to us over the centuries, this was no small claim.

After viewing the portrait and interviewing Hooper, I wrote an article that appeared on the front page of *The Toronto Star's* Saturday Magazine section. A coloured photograph of Hooper's painting accompanied the article, under the headline, "The Real Face of Jesus?"

History has not left us with any portraits or images of Jesus, which is not surprising. Graven images were proscribed by Mosaic law as manifestations of pagan luxury that could lead to idolatry. As a result, the first two centuries of Christianity contributed not at all to the artistic culture of the Roman Empire. Certainly scripture has not left us an account of Jesus' physical appearance. In any event, as art historian Thomas F. Mathews suggests, the scripture's claims for Christ far exceed visual symbols.[1] How, he asks. is the artist to deal with Christ's own self-portrait: "Before Abraham was, I am" or "He who seen me has seen the Father" or "I am the Alpha and the Omega" (Cf. John 8:58, 14:90; Rev. 1:8).

Over the centuries, however, sculptors, painters, glaziers, and mosaic workers have wrestled with putting form to an idea—with some unusual, even incongruous, results. Some of the great Renaissance paintings show Jesus and his contemporaries in clothing more appropriate to Italian courtiers than to first-century Palestinian inhabitants of Galilee, and in settings far removed from the Middle East. With poetic license, artists have painted Jesus with the features of a Caucasian, an Asiatic, or an African, rather than those of a Semite.

Had Hooper managed to do what he claimed? Could that be the true face of Jesus staring out of the canvas in an Ontario Anglican church? Was that how Jesus looked not long before he suffered the slow, brutal, humiliating death of crucifixion?

These questions sparked unusual interest, even among my sceptical *Toronto Star* colleagues, whose comments ranged from the flippant, "He looks like a biker," to the thoughtful, "He does look like a man with a mission." Judging from the number of letters I received, the portrait also struck a cord with many *Toronto Star* readers. For some, Hooper's likeness matched their own idea of what Jesus looked like. Others said the artist was way off the mark. A woman from a small Ontario town complained that Hooper had got it all wrong: "I have seen him [Jesus] and I can describe him," she wrote. She never did follow up with a description.

A Toronto Anglican woman said the portrait confirmed her long-held belief that the blonde, blue-eyed image of Jesus that she had seen so many times in religious paintings was a fiction. She hoped Hooper's portrait would enlighten some of her fellow Anglicans who were convinced that Jesus looked like a Western man, and was, more than likely, also an Anglican.

From the reaction to the article, it appeared that even after two thousand years, Jesus Christ still aroused enough interest to make the headlines. It also supported the view of widespread "illiteracy" when it comes to things biblical: that faith is often based on the un-questioning acceptance of pronounced "truths."

The quest for the historical Jesus—the person of history as distinct from the figure of faith—has taken many twists and turns. The aim of this book, written with the interested layperson in mind, is to cut through some of the theological and scholarly jargon clothing the issue. And, in so doing, to provide signposts to further reading. It is the result of collaboration between New Testament scholar Michael Steinhauser, a believing Christian, and myself, a secular journalist, trained to be something of a "doubting Thomas," who feels comfortable with the label "agnostic." It is also the result of a lot of research, reading, interviewing, and reflection. Although my co-author and I view Jesus differently, we have tried to be as balanced as possible. It hasn't been easy. How does one do justice to disparate scholarly claims? How does one argue with faith? How does one respond to "The church is a mystery" or "It's a matter of faith" or "The Bible says so"?

Quests for the historical Jesus have always sent tremors through Christianity. For those who have carried a comfortable, reassuring Sunday school image of Jesus into maturity, the mere suggestion that this image is false, or at least grossly distorted, is disturbing. Scholars' insistence that true research demands the separation of fact and faith can be threatening.

There is a distinction between fact and faith. "You can't make faith into history. 'Jesus was a Jew' is a statement of fact. 'Jesus was divine' is a statement of belief."[2] And that, for many people, is what the current interest and quest is all about: winnowing some grains of fact from the accumulation of faith. This is not, they point out, an attack on faith. They simply believe that the Jesus of creed and doctrine alone can no longer command the unexamined assent of those who have seen the heavens through Galileo's telescope or examined microbes under a microscope.

This is not to deny that Jesus Christ, Messiah, Saviour and Lord—whatever people call him—may be viewed through the telescope of faith, theology, and creeds. But the historical Jesus, the man in the scarlet robe, must also be viewed through the finest lenses of contemporary reason and research. Some people, finding the search exhilarating, respond with a fervent "Amen." Others, finding it disruptive and threatening, shout "Heresy."

Michael McAteer
Toronto
March 1996

The Colour of Truth 1

S onoma, California, is about an hour's drive north of San Francisco's Golden Gate Bridge. Located in a fertile grape-growing
region that has made California wine world famous, the small, pleas-
ant town still retains some of the flavour of the nineteenth-century
Spanish mission from whence it grew.

One of Sonoma's claims to fame (or infamy, depending on which
side of the theological divide you stand) is that it was, from 1984 to
1995, the home of the Westar Institute, sponsors of the controversial
Jesus Seminar.[1] Lauded by some as being in the vanguard of biblical
scholarship, the Jesus Seminar has also been branded as a diabolical
plot to drive a stake through the very heart of Christendom, thus
attributing more power and authority to the Seminar group than its
members would consider claiming for it.

Enlightened research or tool of Satan? Whatever it is, there's one
sure thing: the Jesus Seminar has put a powerful new twist in the
scholarly search for the historical Jesus. Leaving their lecture halls
and quiet studies to gather twice a year in various locations, the biblical and theological scholars of the Seminar have conducted the search
in the full, probing light of public scrutiny. Rather than being shy of
publicity, the scholars welcome, even court, it. Why?

This courting of publicity has to do with biblical scholar Robert Funk's efforts to address what he saw as widespread biblical illiteracy. Funk established the Westar Institute in 1980 as "an advocate for literacy in Bible and religion." It is a private, non-profit research body, unaffiliated with any religious institution, and it claims to be "theologically neutral." Funk was ordained into the conservative Disciples of Christ Church and turned his talents to academic pursuits soon after. A former Harvard professor, he gave up a position at the prestigious Vanderbilt University to found a Biblical Studies department at the University of Montana. After thirty-three years of college, seminary, and graduate school teaching, he retired to devote himself full time to the Westar Institute and the pursuit of the historical Jesus.

In 1985, Funk and John Dominic Crossan, another noted biblical scholar, convened what they called the Jesus Seminar to embark on a new assessment of the Gospels, including the recently discovered Gospel of Thomas. It was to be, in Funk's words, a clarion call to enlightenment. "The level of public knowledge about biblical matters borders on the illiterate," he said. Drugstore books and magazines play on the fears and ignorance of the uninformed. Radio and television evangelists indulge in platitudes and pieties. In contrast, the Jesus Seminar is for those who prefer facts to fancies, history to histrionics, science to superstition where Jesus and the gospels are concerned.[2]

For Funk, scholars had for too long isolated themselves in quiet libraries and private sanctuaries, burying "their considered views of Jesus and the gospels in technical jargon and in obscure journals." It was time to quit the library, to speak up and go public. Which is just what the Jesus Seminar did.

Starting with thirty scholars, the biblical think-tank eventually grew to more than two hundred, more or less divided between established academic scholars (they are called fellows) and interested non-specialists (associates.) These fellows, says Marcus Borg,[3] reflect a spectrum of contemporary scholarship. Requirements for member-

2

ship are formal, not ideological: typical qualification is a Ph.D. in relevant areas of gospel research. Most are professors in universities, colleges, and seminaries. Almost all are from North America and most are men, because there are relatively few women working in the discipline.

Borg says Seminar fellows also reflect the spectrum of mainstream Christian denominations. Though the Seminar has no connection to any church body, and no record of church membership of fellows is made, he guesses that there are about equal numbers of Catholics, Protestant, and non-religious members. Many are ordained. A few Jewish scholars have been involved. While fundamentalist scholars are welcome, none have become members, presumably because their understanding of scripture as a "divine product" makes the activity of the Seminar "unnecessary and irrelevant and perhaps even blasphemous." A few Southern Baptist scholars did take part in the seminar until pressure from within their denomination forced them to withdraw.

The Jesus Seminar's first major undertaking was to assess the veracity of words and statements attributed to Jesus by the Gospel writers. The leading question was: Did Jesus actually say everything he was purported to have said in the Gospels? Or did the Gospels' authors put words in his mouth to boost the fledgling new religion of Christianity, or to reflect their own views about its founder? At their twice yearly meetings, these gospel specialists examined some fifteen hundred versions of the 503 sayings ascribed to Jesus in the Gospels. After the presentation of papers, discussion and debate, seminar fellows voted, using a archaic voting method. Although dismissed as bizarre and hokey by critics, this voting method certainly captured media and public attention. Seminar members dropped a red, pink, grey, or black bead into a small covered box that was passed from hand to hand. Red meant "That's Jesus"; Pink, "Sure sounds like him"; Grey, "Well maybe"; and Black, "No way. There's been some mistake." So it went, point by point, vote after vote.

One of the first major products of all this discussion and voting was the publication of *The Five Gospels: The Search for the Authentic Words of Jesus.* To cries of outrage from conservative Christians and sniffs of disapproval from other biblical scholars, the Seminar concluded that no more than 20 percent of the sayings attributed to Jesus were uttered by him. This was certainly alarming, and, in at least once instance, radically so. In the Seminar's version of the Lord's Prayer, the words "Our Father" are the only ones to receive a Red vote signifying that these two words, and these two words alone, are the authentic words of Jesus.

Like wheat before a scythe, other dearly held beliefs were cut down. Did Jesus commission his followers to establish a church or inaugurate a world mission? "No," said the Seminar. Ditto with the belief that he selected twelve of his disciples and appointed leaders among them. *The Five Gospels* sent shock waves through the Christian community. And that was only a beginning.

For Christians who accept the Bible as the inerrant voice of God in print, there was more ominous news: The Jesus Seminar turned its attention to the deeds and events in Jesus' life, threatening to question some of the very basic beliefs of the Christian faith. Did Jesus eat a final meal with his disciples in which he interpreted the bread and wine as his body and blood? Did Jesus feed five thousand with five loaves and two fish? "No" on both counts, said the Seminar. Does the story of Judas' betrayal reflect a historical event? "Fiction," said the Seminar. Did Jesus permit a woman to anoint him at a public meal? "Unlikely," said the Seminar, giving it a "grey" vote.

As for that bedrock of Christian belief, the traditional Easter story of Jesus' resurrection, the Seminar concluded that claims of Jesus' resurrection were statements of faith, not reports of a historical events. In probing the issues surrounding this central tenet of Christian belief, it was agreed that Jesus' resurrection was not open to empirical verification. As Marcus Borg put it, a video camera present at one of Jesus' post-resurrection appearances would not have recorded anything on tape.[4]

In March 1989, biblical scholars from across North America gather in Sonoma for a Jesus Seminar spring meeting. For many it's a first, sweet taste of spring, a blessed respite from the slush and bone-chilling cold of less temperate northern climates. An evening buffet awaits them at the Westar Institute, where Funk greets them holding a glass of California wine. There's good fellowship in the air. It's rather like a school reunion as friendships are renewed, news and gossip exchanged. Groups form around the room. In one corner, John Crossan and Julian Hills are the centre of attention. Crossan, professor of Bible Studies at Chicago's DePaul University, is a former Roman Catholic priest and author of the much-discussed and much-debated *The Historical Jesus: The Life of a Mediterranean Jewish Peasant.*

Along with Funk, Crossan has been vilified by the Christian right for his "unorthodox" conclusions about Jesus, and he can tell about some very interesting unsolicited mail he receives. One of the more interesting letters stated that if hell had not been created already, it would have to be created just for him. He appears unfazed by the insult and admits that most of his mail is positive.[5]

Hills, professor at Milwaukee's Marquette University, offers a counter-point to Crossan's exuberance. He's reserved and thoughtful as the informal discussion centres around the question of Jesus' miracles. Could it be that the most primitive form of transmitting the words and deeds of Jesus was by "lists" of sayings or lists of miracles? Hills has investigated several types of lists in early Christianity. It has been suggested that communities passed down summaries of Jesus' miracles as part of their rule of faith. Other lists, he says, contain summaries of doctrine illustrated by miracles, and these were used in instructing new Christian converts.[6] An outsider listening to all this would find it very arcane. Someone asks about a baseball score and brings the discussion down to earth.

The next morning, the scholars gather for business in a large hall around a U-shaped table. No one appears to be in a great hurry to get started. "Where's Ron "Black-bead" Cameron?" someone asks. "We can't begin without Ron. Was he held up at the barbeque?" (Cameron likes to relax on his deck in the summer and cook on the barbeque; he jokingly calls it his "deck" ministry.) There's an outburst of laughter. Cameron, professor at Wesleyan University, is a native of Wyoming. Highly respected by his fellow Seminar members, he is nevertheless often teased for his love of food and the numerous "black" votes he casts at Seminar meetings. There's more good-natured ribbing when Cameron finally arrives, cup of coffee in hand.

Mahlon Smith from Rutgers University enters the room and takes his place at the table, as do Bernard Brandon Scott from Phillips Graduate School in Tulsa, Philip Sellew from the University of Minnesota, Heinz Guenther and John Kloppenborg from the Toronto School of Theology, Robert Miller from Midway College, and Karen King from Occidental College, one of the few female Seminar members.

The presence of film director Paul Verhoeven adds an exotic touch. The Jesus Seminar has been retained by Brooksfilms as a consultant for a proposed new Jesus movie. The film will be directed by Verhoeven, whose credits include such moves as *Robocop*, *Total Recall*, *Basic Instinct*, and *Showgirls*. On the surface, Verhoeven appears to be an unlikely person to direct a movie about Jesus Christ. Because of the violence and raw sex in many of the films he has directed, it has been suggested that a movie about Jesus under his direction will make Martin Scorsese's controversial *The Last Temptation of Christ* look like *The Love Bug*. Yet the Dutch-born director, a non-Christian with no formal religious upbringing, is very serious about the project. He attends every Seminar meeting, except when he is on a film site or in a Hollywood editing room.

Verhoeven plans to make a film called *Christ the Man* to "clarify things that have been covered up for two thousand years." He promises a film that will be "more rough, more crude, more realistic" than any of the Jesus films of the past. "The church has been changing Jesus' message so that the messenger [the church] has become the message," he says. "It's a big mistake. We are all facing the same questions that Jesus must have had when he was led away to his crucifixion and his death."[7]

Meanwhile, as the chairman of the day tries to bring the meeting to order, the media peppers Funk with questions. "Wait, wait, one minute," Funk appeals to the chair. "Can we get a picture for the press?" Ever aware of the value of publicity, Funk has told Seminar members that "sound byte" is among the phrases they should add to their vocabulary: "We have to learn how to give material to the press and television. They're all lazy and aren't going to read the books themselves, so we've got to summarize and reduce our work to what sounds like naive and stupid statements in order to get into the newspapers."

Encouraged by Funk's appeal, photographers move about the table shooting pictures. Scholars mug for the camera. Someone tells Cameron to take the coffee cup out of his face. There's a lot of laughter. The photographers leave and the meeting finally gets underway.

The focus of this meeting is on a passage from Mark's Gospel that deals with the signs of the end of the world and Jesus' second coming:

> But in those days, after that suffering, the sun will be darkened, the moon will not give its light, and the stars will be falling from heaven, and the powers in the heavens will be shaken. And then they will see the Son of man coming in clouds with great powers and glory. And then he will send out the angels, and gather his elect from the four winds, from the ends of the earth to the ends of heaven (Mark 13:24-27).

It's a rather sober, somber topic for a sunny California morning, but the scholars press on with gusto. A speaker suggests that the imagery concerning the darkening of the earth and other cosmic events is not unique to Jesus but is actually typical apocalyptic language— language and imagery used to describe the end of the world. One can find similar scenarios in the Old Testament: the Books of Daniel, Isaiah, and Ezekiel are examples. In fact, the speaker notes, the same imagery appears in New Testament writing harking back to the Old Testament without reference to Jesus. He refers to passages in the Acts of the Apostles and in Paul's letter to the Thessalonians.[8]

The speaker urges his colleagues to vote "black," suggesting that there is little evidence Jesus ever spoke the words attributed to him by Mark. There is a shuffling of papers. Bibles are opened and pages turned as scholars check the text. An animated discussion follows. What about the reference to the Son of man? This is a pivotal passage. For decades scholars have argued that the prediction about the Son of man does not identify Jesus as that figure. Most Seminar scholars appear to agree that the prediction was supplied by Mark for his readers, relating Jesus to prophecy, and is not something Jesus told his disciples decades earlier. The discussion becomes more heated. Did Jesus speak about the Son of man as a messianic figure other than himself? Some of the scholars share this view, but the majority reject it as unsupported by data.

Sitting quietly among his colleagues, Funk watches and listens. He sees trends and patterns developing. From time to time he stirs the pot and appeals to the chair to have Seminar members vote on broader questions. Did Jesus expect the world to end soon? Did Jesus expect to return and usher in a new age? Did Jesus have a forewarning of his death or predict his death as told by Mark? Did Jesus speak of himself as Messiah?

Funk is prodding his colleagues to "quit the library and go public"—to take a stand. They do. Beads are dropped into boxes and votes are tallied. The view that Jesus expected the world to end momentarily, made "popular" by Albert Schweitzer nearly a century ago, has died a scholarly death. The grave has been dug by a whopping 99 percent of these biblical scholars. A similar majority holds the view that Jesus did not expect to return and usher in a new age, not now or in the distant future. And so it goes. Sayings held dear by many Christians as "gospel truth" are discarded as insertions by the Gospel writers. Another Jesus Seminar meeting ends.

As they scan the news wire services, editors across North America get the message from an Associated Press story headlined, "Jesus never said he'd return, scholars say." The story, stripped of theological language and written for the man in the street, says the Gospel writers and later Christians were the ones who predicted a second coming and that Jesus would have been appalled at becoming a cult figure in a new religion. The story adds that the Jesus Seminar also agreed that the language used to describe the future kingdom of God in the New Testament is mythic and symbolic, and recommended that people should not believe in the second coming and a new age. Funk is reported as saying the Seminar's stand did not contradict the faith in God expressed in the Apostles Creed but was at odds with many traditional Christian beliefs.

"At odds with many traditional Christians beliefs" was putting it mildly. By the time *The Five Gospels* was published in late 1993, the Seminar had just about eviscerated the New Testament. Among the conclusions: Jesus did not teach his disciples the Lord's Prayer; his conversations with his disciples at the Last Supper did not likely take place as written; and, while hanging on the cross, Jesus did not ask God to forgive his persecutors.

For Funk and his colleagues, the publication of *The Five Gospels* culminated six years of arduous work, labouring over the sayings attributed to Jesus as recorded in surviving copies of the Gospels and gospel fragments that can be dated prior to A.D. 325. This cut-off date was chosen because it was in this year that Constantine convened the Council of Nicaea, when the "orthodox party solidified its hold on the Christian tradition and other wings of the Christian movement were choked off." So all the surviving gospels and reports, from the first Christian writings to the early decades of the fourth century, were inventoried, not just the canonical Gospels we have today. In other words, Seminar fellows refused to "privilege the gospels that came to be regarded as canonical by the church."[9]

The book's publication was a milestone on the road that the Jesus Seminar had chosen for itself. The book received enormous publicity and was to become a best-seller, appearing for months on the Publisher's Weekly religious best-seller list. A full page advertisement in *The New York Times* Book Review section announcing its publication described it as a "major work that may forever change the way we view Jesus."

Publisher's hype or valid claim? Not surprisingly, Roy Hoover, professor at Whitman College and co-author of *The Five Gospels*, supported the latter view. "The comprehensiveness of this study is unprecedented and is the first cause for celebration," he said. "Surprising though it may seem, a truly comprehensive examination of every statement attributed to Jesus in the ancient sources has never been done before. Previous studies of Jesus' teaching have considered some of the evidence. But no previous study has considered it all and published an informed assessment of it all."

Proclaiming the dawn of a new era in New Testament scholarship, Hoover said *The Five Gospels* brought the historical Jesus into sharper focus. It begged an answer to a crucial question: If Jesus was not a divine being sent into the world to die for our sins, and if he was not the proclaimer of the imminent end of the world and the day of final judgement, than who was he? As for critics of the Jesus Seminar, Hoover said they still have their feet planted in an era of scholarship whose ground has shifted without their knowledge or permission.[10]

The hostile reaction to *The Five Gospels* was not unexpected. In a keynote address to the Jesus Seminar's 1994 spring meeting in Santa Rosa, Funk acknowledged that, while some people were overjoyed at the "understanding and release it provides," others lamented the book's appearance as Satan's work. Hailing the book's publication as a historic milestone in the search for the historical Jesus, Funk said the roots of *The Five Gospels* can be traced to the rediscovery of the parables of Jesus three decades ago, when biblical scholars abandoned metaphorical interpretation of the parables and saw in them the language of Jesus addressed to the age in which he lived. "A trickle of interest in the language of Jesus during the 1960s became a torrent in the 1970s and a flood in the 1980s," he said. "It is now apparent that we have come to the end of an epoch in gospel studies inaugurated almost a century ago by Johannes Weiss, Albert Schweitzer, Rudolph Bultmann, and Karl Barth."

Paying tribute to these great German biblical scholars, Funk said they put a "period" to the nineteenth century and launched the twentieth. "We are surprised that we suddenly find ourselves at the end of the twentieth century quest for Jesus," he said. "We are being carried along by a new movement of national, even international, dimensions as we face a new era in biblical scholarship."

Others begged to differ, and did so most vociferously. This was hardly unexpected. As far back as 1906, Albert Schweitzer cautioned that scholars must be "prepared to find that the historical knowledge of the personality and life of Jesus will not be a help, but perhaps even an offense to religion."[11]

When Funk launched the Jesus Seminar, he told charter members their objective was to "inquire simply, rigorously after the voice of Jesus, after what he really said," and cautioned that the search could lead them into tempestuous, even dangerous, waters: "In this process, we will be asking a question that borders the sacred, that even abuts blasphemy, for many in our society. As a consequence, the course we shall follow may prove hazardous. We may well provoke hostility. But we will set out, in spite of the dangers, because we are professionals and because the issue of Jesus is there to be faced."[12]

And there was hostility. Seminar members have been vilified, sneered at, derided, and damned. The Seminar has been dismissed as a self-appointed supreme court of second-rate, liberal, Protestant scholars out to propagate a politically correct version of Jesus. As a conservative American Episcopal priest put it, the Jesus Seminar's work

servative American Episcopal priest put it, the Jesus Seminar's work was nothing more than a sloppy rehash of existing ideas. Claiming that most Christians, including religious leaders, had no doubt about the validity of the Gospels or of the words attributed to Jesus, a Southern Baptist minister slammed Seminar scholars for attempting to pass off "a liberal theological agenda" as legitimate scholarship. "I'll take Funk's word that no evil was intended by this," the minister said. "But after they get done, the only thing that is left is a liberal Jesus, a politician running for office who says a lot of things we want to hear."[13]

In a letter to the editor responding to a *Toronto Star* article on the Jesus Seminar, David Burrows, a rural Ontario Anglican priest summed up his feelings in one word: "Baloney." Did you ever, he asked, hear of scientific conclusions that had to be voted on? "That's what the Jesus Seminar is doing, isn't it? Can you imagine Albert Einstein getting up before his colleagues at the University of Zurich in 1909 and saying, "All right, how many votes in favour of $E=mc^2$? This is not science, neither is the Jesus Seminar."

"Ludicrous," said Schuyler Brown, a New Testament scholar at Toronto's University of St. Michael's College, in another letter to the editor. "The idea of a group of New Testament scholars taking a vote to determine the historicity of sayings attributed to Jesus is so ludicrous that, if I had not read it in the *Star*, I would have assumed that someone had made it up as a joke. But scholarly hubris is no joke. It gives a bad name to serious study of the New Testament. Moreover, in trying to confer data base irreformability upon its own pronouncements, the Jesus Seminar is imitating the very dogmatism that the historical critical approach to biblical interpretation arose to challenge."

"Blasphemy," cried a group of Canadian Salvation Army members, as they wrote to the *Star's* editor, warning of divine retribution. "Christians believe the Bible to be the inspired word of God. Archaeology is constantly uncovering facts which point out the authenticity of this Holy Book. The Bible has stood the test of time, both in the veracity of its content, and in providing a pattern for a successful, Christ-filled life. 'Cult figure' and 'wandering sage' fall lightly from the lips but Divine retribution will not fall as lightly on those who blaspheme. We will pray for you. Yes, one hundred biblical scholars will come and go but as it is stated in Isaiah 40:8: 'The grass withereth and flowers fadeth but the word of God shall stand forever.'"

While the Jesus Seminar's work has been described as possibly the most revolutionary movement in Christianity since the Reformation,[14] others dismiss it as a flash in the pan with no lasting impact. Jerome Neyrey, a Jesuit priest and professor of Theology at the University of Notre Dame, suggests it will go virtually unnoticed by most. "The people who sit in church on Sunday undergo a continuing socialization process that reinforces the readings and homilies they're exposed to," he says. "That means those books will make a bit of a splash, but I don't think people will be talking about them three years from now." The prominent and respected English theologian N. Thomas Wright agrees, dismissing the Seminar's work as "a bit of a nine-days wonder that will eventually run out of red, pink, black, and grey things to do."[15]

Calling *The Five Gospels* "a mess of the first order," John Meier a Catholic priest, noted biblical scholar, and one of the key players in contemporary historical Jesus research, says Jesus Seminar members are trying to take a terribly inexact study and give it scientific neatness. "They've painted themselves into a corner with their extreme scepticism. If they do make a movie, it will be the shortest in history."[16]

Others are as equally dismissive, calling the Seminar's work flawed, ideological, doctrinaire, extremist, and lightweight. One of the most scathing attacks was launched by Richard Hays, associate professor of New Testament at The Divinity School, Duke University, North Carolina. He not only questions the Seminar's criteria for judgement but also accuses the Seminar's co-founders as being charlatans. Noting that *The Five Gospels* is dedicated to Galileo Galilei, Thomas

Jefferson, and David Friedrich Strauss, Hays suggests the dedication left out one figure "who might most appropriately symbolize the public face of this project: P. T. Barnum." The co-chairmen, Robert Funk and John Dominic Crossan, had demonstrated, Hays says, an ingenuity for promotion that would surely have warmed the heart of that master American showman.

As Hays sees it, the Seminar's "operative methodology" is so seriously flawed that it inevitably produces a skewed portrait of Jesus' teachings and—contrary to the impression fostered by *The Five Gospels*—its conclusions represent the "idiosyncratic opinions of one particular faction of critical scholars." That Seminar participants are not without credentials, holding doctorates from reputable institutions, is beside the point. The point is that "this imaginative book has been produced by a self-selected body of scholars who hold a set of unconventional views about Jesus and the gospels. They are, of course, free to publish these views; however, their attempt to present these views as 'the assured results of critical scholarship' is—one must say it—reprehensible deception."[17]

Just before leaving for a sabbatical at Jerusalem's L'Ecole Biblique in 1994, Terrance Prendergast, a Jesuit priest and New Testament scholar who was later appointed one of Toronto's auxiliary bishops, picked up a copy of *The Five Gospels* and expressed his dismay at what the Seminar had done to the Gospels. Turning to Mark's Gospel as it appears in *The Five Gospels*, Prendergast noted that there is hardly anything there belonging to Jesus, even though Mark is supposed to be the first Gospel written. "When my students go through the Gospel of Mark in this book and find only a few words in red, they wonder what scholarship is doing," he said. "There is an authority to this book that is not deserved, and it claims more than it can deliver. The whole body of scholarship continues to work on such issues as the historical Jesus and some scholars are letting the Jesus Seminar have the last word on the matter."

While not without merit—"engaging, provocative and never dull"—*The Five Gospels*, by Prendergast's assessment, is "fatally flawed, captive to an ideology more doctrinaire than the one it intends to displace." He suggests that in its determination to replace a naive fundamentalism found in New Testaments that colour all of Jesus' sayings red, the Jesus Seminar may ironically be establishing an even more insidious kind of fundamentalism. What's more, the Seminar's portrait of Jesus "cuts him off from both Judaism and the Christian church." What's left, suggests Prendergast, is "a gadfly who was witty, enjoyed a good time, was bright and intelligent, who wanted to over- turn society and create a society where everybody was equal and had access to God without mediation. Someone has suggested that this Jesus looks a little like Jesus Seminar members."[18]

Or, suggests John Meier, "a tweedy poetaster who spent his time spinning parables and Japanese koans, a literary aesthete who toyed with 1st-century deconstructionism, or a bland Jesus who simply told people to look at the lilies of the field—such a Jesus would threaten no one, just as the university professors who create him threaten no one."[19]

However, Robert Bater, a United Church of Canada minister, New Testament scholar, and Jesus Seminar member, argues that the sheer weight of new material is forcing many theologians to refashion their outlook. "Those who cannot accommodate the new Jesus are in for a great shock," he says. "I have a strong sense we are in a situation not unlike the battle over evolution." For Bater, the portrait of Jesus that is emerging is that of a prophet, a sage, and a very worldly person, at home with the poor and the rejected. And those most concerned about orthodoxy have often played down his humanity. "He was so human, so surprisingly human, and such an astute observer of what was going on about him," he says. "I don't think that Christ thought of himself as a divine being."[20]

Another United Church minister, Daniel Bogert-O'Brien, has defended the Seminar against increasing attacks from both Christian fundamentalists and middle-of-the-road scholars who find their own views overshadowed by the glaring light of publicity focused on the Seminar. Bogert-O'Brien, who helped arrange the Seminar's 1991 fall meeting in Edmonton, is surprised by the strength of the criticism. He notes that the Edmonton meeting was ecumenical in scope, sponsored by university chaplains from the United, Anglican, and Christian Reform churches, as well as the university's Religious Studies department of the United Church's St. Stephen's College and the Roman Catholic St. Joseph's College.

Describing the Jesus Seminar as a collection of scholars representing mainline scholarship, Bogert-O'Brien says that while some people may find some of the Seminar's conclusions unpalatable, they are old hat to him and other United Church ministers, who heard them years ago in seminary. Unfortunately, the new insights into Jesus had not being shared with the people in the pew. "We clergy have been the stumbling block to meaningful conversation with scholarship," he says. "What the Jesus Seminar is doing is good scholarship. Bad scholarship is saying: 'We have all the answers and that's all there is to it.'"[21]

But for conservative Christians, it's more fundamental than a matter of good or bad scholarship. What is at stake is the veracity of the Bible, the very bedrock of their Christian faith. So, when the Jesus Seminar states that the Christian Gospels are now assumed to be narratives in which the memory of Jesus is embellished by mythic elements and stories that express the church's faith in him, the reaction is swift and strong.

For Graham Scott, United Church minister and a prominent spokesman for the Church's conservative wing, Jesus Seminar scholars have reduced the faith to their "own very reductionist consensus." Nevertheless, he believes that despite all their efforts, the power of Jesus continues to shine through. Recalling the film *Jesus of Montreal*, Scott notes that "the sources used there were just atrocious. And yet the power of Jesus appeared to come through anyway: "Generally speaking, Jesus manages to get through an awful lot of garbage. He has the power to get through even the most meagre presentation. And the Jesus Seminar conclusions are the meagrest by far."[22]

As the Jesus Seminar continued to attract unprecedented media attention, the conservative backlash intensified. Under the headline "Pundits with Pebbles: Why We Believe in the Virgin Birth," Timothy George, writing in the conservative *Christianity Today*, accused the Jesus Seminar of tossing stones at the glass house of faith. Christians do not know or need to know the "how" of Jesus' birth, he said, taking the Seminar to task for voting against faith. "Ostensibly based on 'factual empirical evidence,' (how does one research a first-century woman's virginity anyway?) the conclusions of the Jesus Seminar are really a rehash of old canards long since dealt with by responsible scholars of Christian origins," George wrote. "Jesus Seminar scholars would have us believe the birth of Jesus is just another of the pagan stories of gods and demigods, involving as they do sordid liaisons between Olympian deities and mortal women."

Turning to the second-century Justin Martyr for support, George suggested that the pagan convert to Christianity, who became an influential church thinker, is a more reliable theological guide than any clutch of Jesus Seminar scholars. That early theologian, he said, saw the real difference between pagan myths and reality when he wrote that the "Holy Spirit by whom the Virgin Mary became pregnant was none other than the eternal God who came upon Mary and overshadowed her, causing her to be with child not by intercourse but by power."[23]

However, scholar Mahlon Smith, professor for New Testament at Rutgers University, takes issue with this line of reasoning. Addressing those who cast stones, he defends the work of the Jesus Seminar, advising those who shun criticism to avoid biblical interpretation: "Criticism goes with biblical turf. There are always those who distrust the motives, the methods, and the results of biblical scholarship

17

of whatever stripe. Censure and invective come as often from the learned elite as from a poorly informed public."

That the Jesus Seminar has been railed at in the "pulpit, press and ivory tower" is neither surprising nor the cause of undue alarm, Smith says. The extent of the criticism may, in fact, be an occasion to rejoice, indicating as it does that the Seminar is reaching a wider audience than first anticipated. However, the rejoicing is tempered by "the amount of misinformation, false allegations, and just plain invective" that punctuates the criticism. We cannot smother the uproar but we can seek to show that charges leveled against us are distortions," says Smith.[24]

One of things that trouble Jesus Seminar critics is the amount of publicity generated by the numerically small Seminar. As one critic puts it, the Jesus Seminar is "the creation of a media culture looking for a story," aided and abetted by a small group of scholars. Graham Scott, for instance, points out that the Seminar has about one hundred voting members while the Society of New Testament Studies has one thousand members and the Society for Biblical Literature has five thousand.[25] And yet, this small group of scholars gets all the attention. Why? A lot has to do with how the Jesus Seminar packages its findings.

Dominic Crossan makes no apologies for the Seminar's size or for the unorthodox way it gets its conclusions out via the media. From the start, he says, the Jesus Seminar wanted to go public, to invite the media in, and to let people on the outside in on what was going on. And that broke the well-established rule that biblical scholarship would be carried out in an atmosphere that discourages outside participation.

"The more or less implicit deal was that scholarship would be done in the university, in the learned journals, in the learned societies," Crossan says. "You would not have a clue what was going on even if you read it. But nobody could come after you or attack you. It was a sort of elitist type of scholarship. Going public was breaking the rules. The Jesus Seminar was never intended to be just scholars discussing the historical Jesus." He adds, "It's new for scholars to be going public and to say 'We are going to let you know what we are discussing. We don't think you are so dumb that you won't understand. We'll tell you the main issues and the main arguments. Come into the discussion. It's too important to wait one hundred years until we have decided.'"

Crossan agrees that there is a certain air of flamboyance about the way the Seminar votes. Scholars could more easily vote by simply putting up their hands. But that would be far less exotic than voting with beads, which "plays to the visuals." Crossan recalls that in one meeting when the Seminar was pressed for time and was voting with paper ballots, it bowed to a media request to vote using to the bead method. "We understand that," Crossan says. "That was intended to capture people's visual imagination."[26]

By capturing the public's imagination, conservative Christians fear that the Seminar's conclusions are the only ones being heard in the marketplace. As a result, they have been forced to go on the counter-attack. In 1995, N. Thomas Wright, the English theologian and dean of Lichfield Cathedral, undertook a cross-America speaking tour on the theme "Who was Jesus?" in an effort to counter many of the Jesus Seminar's much-publicized conclusions. The same year saw the publication of several books written by evangelical Christians in defence of the biblical view of Jesus and Christianity.

One such book was *Jesus Under Fire*, subtitled *Modern Scholarship Reinvents the Historical Jesus*,[27] which provided a forum for evangelical scholars concerned about the possible fallout from the Jesus Seminar. J. P. Moreland, professor of philosophy at Talbot School of Theology and one of the book's general editors, stresses the importance of responding to Jesus being reduced to a "minimalistic historical figure" in the name of religious pluralism. If Jesus can be reduced to being a spinner of religious wisdom or a sage or a kind of "politically correct, twentieth-century, Anglo-Saxon, liberal, university professor, into gay rights," then, says Moreland, Jesus is not all that much different from Buddha, leading to the conclusion that "religions all turn out to be the same."

A major complaint of *Jesus Under Fire* contributors and other conservative Christians is this: many contemporary scholars assume that the biblical records are "fictitious" unless and until they can be proven truthful. Conservative biblical scholar Donald Hagner, of Fuller Theological Seminary in Pasadena, complains that the Jesus Seminar adopts an historical-critical methodology which rules out the possibility of the supernatural, "a priori" [existing in the mind prior to and independent of experience]. How, he asks, do we know that God cannot act in the historical process? And if God can in fact act in the historical process, then "perhaps we ought to listen to what these documents [the Gospels] have to say in that connection."[28]

Essentially, the conservative charge is that liberal scholars adopt a "burden of proof" argument, demanding that supposedly historical elements in the Gospels must be demonstrated to be so. This, they claim, leads to the conclusion that all of the activities ascribed to Jesus in the Gospels are assumed not to be true until proven otherwise.

Which is what critical scholarship is all about, Crossan counter-argues: "Public discourse is the issue. By critical I mean you come into public discourse, sit around a table with historians of ancient history, experts on Roman history, who don't give a 'hoot' about Jesus, and say here's my view of Jesus and I defend it as history. If you can't do that, then you are not in public discourse." The Christian faith, says Crossan, does not tell us what we need to know about the historical Jesus. "Christian faith tells us how the historical Jesus (fact) is the manifestation of God for us here and now (interpretation)," he says. "And no amount of faith can turn an interpretation into fact."[29]

Crossan also has an answer for those who criticize the Jesus Seminar for "voting" on the probable authenticity of individual parables and sayings of Jesus. In short, he says, they should know better. Scholars know, even if the laity does not, that the very Greek text of the New Testament on which any modern translation must be based is itself a reconstruction "and the result, however executed, of a scholarly vote is a committee of experts."[30]

Funk supports his colleague, noting that books to be included in the New Testament were determined by vote in various ecclesiastical councils, and those votes were often determined by theological rather than historical considerations. He also chastises those who attack the Seminar for reaching conclusions without taking into account the possibility of the supernatural. Empirical data and the rules of evidence should be scholarly criteria for making judgements. A critical scholar does not "put dogmatic consideration first and insist the actual evidence confirm theological premises." And Seminar scholars, he says, pride themselves on being critical scholars.

Essentially, what the Jesus Seminar is doing, says Funk, is to "relocate Jesus way back there" in his own time and place, far removed from the immediate interests of modern institutions or personal needs. As Albert Schweitzer once put it, Jesus is a stranger to our way of thinking and living. To recover that stranger is, says Funk, the task of those who have devoted their lives to rediscovering the ancient world through its surviving documents and artifacts.

Of course, discussing Jesus in secular terms poses a challenge to traditional images. And when you challenge orthodoxy, there is a price to pay. Funk shrugs it off. The Jesus Seminar, he says, was established to tell the "truth, the historical truth," about Jesus. Who he was, what he said, and what he did. Says Funk: "Fellows and associates of the Jesus Seminar would like to know who Jesus really was. Most people would like to know who he really was. Only by freeing him from the overlay of Christian piety and rhetoric can we hope to discover the profile of that single face in a Galilean crowd."[31]

Questions and Answers 2

"Who do men say that I am?" Like the tolling of a distant church bell calling the faithful to prayer, this question has echoed down the ages since it was first posed by Jesus almost two thousand years ago.

The author of Mark's Gospel tells us that this question was addressed to Jesus' disciples. They answered in a variety of ways as they trod the dry, dusty ground of Palestine with their master. Simple, untutored men, they may well have scratched their heads as they struggled with the question before answering: "John the Baptist, and others say Elijah, and others one of the prophets" (Mark 8:28).

The struggle to answer this pivotal question continues today as new archaeological finds, the discovery of lost ancient texts, and new theological conclusions challenge long-held assumptions, giving fresh impetus to the search for the historical Jesus.

Every couple of years, suggests the University of Chicago's Martin Marty, a well-known and respected professor of Modern Christianity and a senior editor with *The Christian Century*, someone tries to prove that Jesus was a zealot who carried a dagger, or married Mary Magdalene and the French monarchy are their descendants, or that Jesus was a member of a hallucinogenic mushroom-munching cult.

For many devout Christians, there can only be one answer to the question asked so many years ago: Jesus Christ is the Son of God who suffered an agonizing death on a Roman cross and confirmed his divinity by his resurrection from the dead three days later. It's a matter of faith. But others, Christians among them, see Jesus in a different light. Like the disciples of old, they too answer Jesus' question in a variety of ways: inspired teacher, itinerant preacher, leader of a homosexual cult, social revolutionary, disturber of the peace, gadfly, madman, nice guy. Jesus Christ, Superstar! Despite all their probing, historians can still come up with only the blurred figure of a man; elusive and controversial.

Noting the irony, University of Chicago scholar Bernard McGinn says that, historically speaking, the paradox is that we have more material about Jesus and more sayings attributed to him than almost any other figure of his time. And yet there is little agreement about what he may have "really" said or even about the details of his life and ministry.[1] Much of the problem stems from the fact that Jesus himself wrote nothing; the abundant materials about his life are almost universally from "interested" sources; that is, from his own followers. There are only fleeting references in the non-Christian literature of the time to someone who may or may not have been the figure we have come to know as Jesus.

The result is that the images of Jesus that modern scholars construct find their origin, as Paula Fredriksen puts it, in an area where there is no written record or in "that documentary vacuum inhabited by Jesus of Nazareth." So, she says, "no matter how cautious, critical, and self-conscious our methods and modest our claims when attempting to recover him, this 'historical Jesus' is but an image, at best a coherent set of inferences from historical knowledge."[2]

We don't know the year of Jesus' birth. The sixth-century Roman monk and astronomer Dionysius Exiguus, given the task of creating a new calendar based on the year of Jesus' birth rather than on the founding of Rome, is said to have made an error of four to seven years. The result is that rather than being born in A.D. 1 according to our calendar, Jesus was born four or seven years earlier. What did Jesus look like? Was he short or tall, lean or stout? The New Testament is silent about his physical appearance.

German biblical scholar Ethelbert Stauffer concluded, reasonably, that because the New Testament does not give a physical description of Jesus, he did not differ particularly from other Palestinian Jews of his time. Stauffer noted that even Jesus' adversaries were silent about his appearance. "The Rabbis had very definite standards regarding the outward appearance of a proper Jew, especially a teacher," Stauffer wrote. "They could, if occasion demanded, scornfully and harshly decry any deviations from these standards."[3] This means that if we wish to form a picture of Jesus' appearance, we must sketch a Palestinian Jew of the day, supplementing this with the few individual features we can gather from scattered and indirect evidence in the Gospels. Strictly speaking, says University of Essen theologian Uta Ranke-Heineman, we don't know a whole lot more than that he was born, that there were people who followed him as his disciples, and that he was executed on the cross—the Roman version of the gallows—and thus came to a wretched end.[4]

Others flesh out this brief profile: Jesus was born most likely in Nazareth, not Bethlehem, and had four brothers and at least two sisters. Brought up in a pious family of Jewish peasants in lower Galilee, he was attracted to the movement of John the Baptist, the Jordan Valley desert preacher of repentance and proclaimer of the imminence of God's judgement. After being baptized by John the Baptist, Jesus headed out on his own, beginning his two-year public ministry when he was about thirty-three or thirty-four. While in Jerusalem for the approaching feast of the Passover in A.D. 30, he apparently sensed that the increasing hostility between himself and the Jerusalem temple authorities was about to reach a climax. On the Thursday evening of April 6, by today's dating, Jesus celebrated a solemn farewell meal with his inner circle of disciples. Arrested in Gethsemane on the night of April 6, he was examined by some Jewish officials and then handed over on the morning of Friday, April 7, to Pontius Pilate, the governor of Judea, who quickly condemned him to death by crucifixion. After being scourged and mocked, Jesus was crucified outside Jerusalem and was dead by the evening of that same Friday. He was about thirty-six years old.[5]

It's not much on which to build a biography, in our modern sense. Apart from one reference to Jesus as a precocious twelve-year-old in the temple confounding Jewish teachers, found in the Gospel of Luke, there is nothing to tell us about his boyhood, youth, and early manhood. Speculations about these "lost years" have been endless. It has even been suggested that during these years Jesus travelled throughout the world imbibing wisdom, visiting northern India to study Buddhism, living with the Druids in Celtic England, and meditating in Japanese monasteries. Most scholars pay scant attention to these imaginings, dismissing them as the products of inventive minds, however delightful the legends. Of course it is possible that Jesus did travel extensively outside of Palestine. However, historian S. Scott Barkley finds accounts of such travels implausible and unnecessary to explain Jesus' wisdom: "Everything we find in the Jesus tradition we can understand as coming out of the deep roots of the Judaism in which he grew up. So, we don't have any reason to say that he went and learned his non-violence from the Buddhists."[6]

Despite the scantiness of historical data, Ranke-Heinemann believes that Jesus was a man who sought—and found—God; that he wanted to reveal this God as being close to everyone and to make everyone intimate with both God and neighbour. Unfortunately, this Jesus "lies buried not only in Jerusalem, but also beneath a mountain of kitsch, tall tales, and church phraseology. Though he is missing and presumed dead, we must go forth and rediscover him."[7]

No matter how much information we can extract from history, many scholars are convinced there will always be a wide gulf between the Jesus of history (fact) and the Christ of faith (interpretation). English scholar Stewart Sutherland argues that nothing the research historian can come up with will prove or justify Christian faith: no amount of historical knowledge about the life of Jesus of Nazareth will guarantee or verify that he is the Christ, the Son of God.[8]

In a similar vein, the great-hearted Lutheran theologian and pastor Dietrich Bonhoeffer argued that, when one knows all there is to know about Jesus, he remains an ambiguous figure and that no further piece of historical information can remove this ambiguity. Bonhoeffer was one of the most influential theologians of this century, and his writings continue to have wide influence. One of his major works is concerned with the growing secularization of the world and the need to speak about God. Forbidden to teach by the Nazis, he was banned from Berlin and his seminary was closed in 1937. In 1942, he tried to form a link between the Germans opposed to Hitler and the British government. He was arrested the following year and hanged by the Nazis in 1945.

The lack of hard historical evidence about Jesus has resulted in depiction of him that range from "King of Kings" to long-haired, full-bearded hippie with gentle eyes, dressed as a 1960s flower child. There is, as John Meier puts it, "no neutral Switzerland" in the world of Jesus research. Whatever is written is written from some point of view.[9] Inevitably, each opinion is a personal interpretation.

Albert Schweitzer (1875-1965) said much the same thing at the turn of the century. In his monumental work *The Quest of the Historical Jesus* (1906), the scholar, musician, missionary and Nobel Prize recipient cautioned that biographies of Jesus tell us more about the biases, prejudices, and agendas of the biographers than they do about Jesus. One of the pitfalls of historical Jesus research is that scholars searching for Jesus tend to see what they want to see: they look down a well and see their own reflection—the face of a man with whom they can identify.[10]

The face Bruce Barton saw was that of a muscular Christian, a "glad-handing host, Rotarian, speculative promoter and canny businessman." In *The Man Nobody Knows*, published in 1925, Barton, an aggressive American businessman and advertising ace, depicted Jesus as a man who "loved the outdoors, had a great body steeled with hard muscles, and was the most sought-after dinner guest in Jerusalem."[11] In contrast, the Jesus many liberal theologians see is a Jesus so comfortably left-wing and counter-cultural as to be "the ideal Jesus from a Christian secularist point of view."[12] Far from being the meek and mild figure of Sunday school, this Jesus is both healer and social revolutionary—a Jesus without the Lord's Prayer, the Last Supper, the Virgin Birth, or the Sermon on the Mount.

All this searching, probing, and theorizing has led many devoted Christians to believe that the Jesus they once knew has been kidnapped and replaced with a man they would never think of inviting to dinner, especially not Sunday dinner. Each new challenge to dearly held beliefs is met with a mixture of pain, bemusement, and outrage.

None of this is confined to our time. When an article by French novelist Anatole France was published in an anti-clerical newspaper on Christmas Day, 1891, it sent pious matrons of Paris reaching for their scented handkerchiefs. In a fictitious interview with Pontius Pilate in his retirement years, France had the former governor of Judea saying, "Jesus? Jesus of Nazareth? I can't remember him."

As late as 1971, two Pittsburgh shopkeepers felt the sting of a 1794 statute when they were charged with blasphemy. Their crime? They displayed a "wanted" poster for Jesus Christ in the windows of their stores .A long-haired, hippie-likeness of Jesus adorned the poster, which said: "Wanted for sedition, criminal anarchy, vagrancy and conspiracy to overthrow the established government. Dresses poorly; said to be a carpenter by trade; ill-nourished; associates with common working people, unemployed and bums. Alien; said to be a Jew." The charges were dropped after the American Civil Liberties Union came to the shopkeepers' defence.

Challenges by secular sources to traditional images of Jesus, while offensive to many Christians, are often shrugged off as something to be expected from sources perceived to have a built-in, anti-Christian bias. When churches start messing about with traditional views of Jesus, the outcry can be tumultuous. Toronto's Bloor Street United Church found itself into hot water in 1979 when it hosted an inter-church Good Friday service. The service featured an eight-foot sculpture of a naked woman, with arms outstretched in the form of a cross. The sculpture was the focus of the service's theme, "battered women," but the point was lost on some churchgoers, who could see no connection between Good Friday and a naked crucified woman.

"It was the holiest Holy Week we ever had," recalls the Rev. Clifford Elliott, the senior church minister in the eye of the raging storm that led to a heresy charge—later dropped—being brought against him. "It contributed a lot to the whole ongoing search for who was Jesus and who was the Christ. It was a very profound statement and a very positive affirmation for feminists, for the feminism movement in general, and for feminist theology. It helped open people to the idea that God became a human being expressed as a man; that Jesus could just as well have been a woman."[13]

The idea that Jesus was a woman was nothing less than sacrilegious for some Christians. Others praised the church's courage for focusing attention on the social evil of woman battering.

Issues such as this, thrashed out in the media as well as in church circles, serve notice of a wide-spread fascination with the man called Jesus. Having stepped out of churches' stained glass windows, Jesus Christ now walks the streets of Montreal as a contemporary man. And, as Denys Arcand's film *Jesus of Montreal* suggests, the modern Jesus would find survival in today's society as difficult as it was in Roman times.

In its December 1991 issue, *Life* magazine published "exclusive pictures" about the O. J. Simpson case, which had much of North America hooked to the television screen. These pictures appeared inside the magazine. But appearing on the magazine's cover was an artist's impression of what Jesus may have looked like—a pleasant-faced man with shoulder-length brown hair. And inside the magazine, an article headed "Solving the Mystery of Jesus and Why It Matters Today" reported responses, from atheist to fundamentalist Christian, to the question "Who was Jesus?"

"The Bible is the fundamental way to view him. He was man and God," was the unambiguous response of Robert Miller, spokesperson for the Brethren in Christ World Mission. Jon Murray, president of American Atheists, was just as emphatic. "There never was such a person in the history of the world as Jesus Christ," was the atheist's response. "There was no historical, living, breathing, sentient human being by that name. Ever!"

Others were less positive. "I don't think we know who Jesus was," said Peter Bien, professor of English at Dartmouth College, New Hampshire, and translator of Nikos Kazantzaki's *The Last Temptation of Christ.* "The Gospels, which were written for political purposes—to convert people—are after the fact. Fifty years at least." For New York's Roman Catholic Archbishop John Cardinal O'Connor, it was very much a matter of faith: "I don't see how, without the gift of faith, you could believe he was the Son of God. Faith makes the difference. You can study the Scriptures till your eyes fall out, and without the gift of faith you're not going to believe Christ was the Son of God. The miracle is faith itself."

When Tyler Roberts, lecturer and head tutor of Religion at Harvard University, asked his class who Jesus was, most students said he was a religious figure. Some said he was a philosopher, comparing him to the Greek philosopher Socrates. Then there was Jesus as political leader, with one student comparing him to Mao and Stalin.

The description of Jesus as a great teacher who transformed his listeners while alienating the power structure could just as easily fit the Greek philosopher Socrates, who died four centuries before Christ, says Yale University professor Jaroslav Pelikan. Both of them were outstanding teachers who taught and practiced the simple life. Both were regarded as religious renegades, and both were executed. But, as Pelikan notes, nobody has ever built a cathedral in honour of Socrates. "Socrates called upon people to think straight, but with Jesus there's more than just 'teaching,' there's a transcendent dimension, beyond the here and now, as a source of hope and meaning." Having said that, Pelikan also notes that when one considers the Christian tradition of witness to Jesus, "it is not the sameness but the kaleidoscopic variety that is its most conspicuous feature."[14]

If Jesus cast such a shadow over history, why, then, when sifting through its detritus, are we left with so little that tells us about the man and his ministry? Jesus put an indelible stamp on history but the historians of his time hardly noticed. Non-Christian references to Jesus are so meagre as to be almost non-existent. From the viewpoint of the Jewish and pagan literature of the century following Jesus, he was, as John Meier puts it, at most a "blip" on the radar screen. Difficult as it is may be for the devout but unreflective Christian to accept, "Jesus was simply insignificant to national and world history as seen through the eyes of Jewish and pagan historians of the first and early second centuries. If seen at all, it was at the periphery of their vision."[15]

One might expect that the most likely source of information about Jesus would be Paul, the only writer of New Testament material who, without doubt, was writing in the early decades after Jesus' death. However, as Meier argues, since the centre of Paul's theology was the death and resurrection of Jesus, his letters to Christian communities "did not aim generally at imparting initial knowledge about Jesus, which was rather presupposed—and recalled only when necessary." We are really left with those "gloriously ambiguous" records—the Gospels attributed to Matthew, Mark, Luke, and John. These four narratives, composed by unknown authors, are the major source of our knowledge about Jesus. Written forty to seventy years after the events they narrate, and despite the "harmony" they may show, they are, as many scholars say, so ridden with inconsistencies that accepting them as historical reports can be problematic.

Mind you, there are those who don't accept that there is any-thing ambiguous about the Gospels. Among them is conservative British Anglican theologian Michael Green, who argues that no books in the world have been so thoroughly scrutinized and validated as the four Gospels. He further argues that these records present a re-markable harmony in the picture they paint of Jesus that suggests their authors were not working in collusion or inventing what they wrote. "The artless, unplanned harmony in their accounts is impres-sive and convincing," says Green. "What we read in the gospels chimes in both with the secular evidence about Jesus and with what the apostle Paul has to say writing a decade before the earliest gospels. Who could have made that picture up? The figure they represent is so dif-ferent from anyone else, so sublime, so challenging. These men were writing fact, not fiction."[16]

Edward Stillingford, the seventeenth-century Anglican Bishop of Worchester, argued much the same way when he wrote, "There is no greater evidence of any history in the world than there is that all the things reported in the New Testament were done at the time they are pretended to be." It was inconceivable, the bishop argued, that a dozen "rude, mean, obscure, illiterate, simple men could have over-come the customs and power of the whole world save by supernatu-ral aid."[17]

Conservative theologian Craig Blomberg acknowledges that the teachings of Jesus were not written down at the time he spoke them but were initially preserved orally. Because of this, they were "para-phrased, abbreviated, combined together in small collections" before ultimately being put into their familiar form by the Gospel writers. The fact that Jesus spoke in Aramaic while the Gospels were written in Greek means that "literal translation from one language to another inevitably breaks down at numerous points." However, Blomberg says conservative Christians believe that the writing of the Gospels was done "under the superintendence of the Holy Spirit, and through His inspiration the writers accurately reported exactly what he wanted them to represent of the life and teachings of Jesus."[18]

But conservative Christians who root their faith in the inerrancy of scripture appear to be swimming against a strong tide of mainstream New Testament scholarship. For decades, liberal Protestant scholars have presented the Gospels as literary, rather than historical, records. In a 1994 statement, the Vatican added its weight to that position. While recognizing the Gospels as the inspired word of God, the Vatican acknowledged that they were written by human authors possessed of limited capacities and resources. Calling the fundamentalist approach to scripture "a kind of intellectual suicide," the Vatican noted that the Gospels were written years after Jesus spoke, when "there was no stenographer, no one with a tape recorder on at the time."[19]

When we turn to non-Christian references to Jesus, they are more problematic and even less helpful. There is, for instance, the well-known reference to Jesus in the pages of *Jewish Antiquities*, written about A.D. 93 by the Jewish historian Flavius Josephus (A.D. 37/38– ca. 100):

> About this time there lived Jesus, a wise man, if indeed one ought to call him a man. For he was as one who wrought surprising feats and was a teacher of such people as accept the truth gladly. He won over many Jews and many Greeks. He was the Messiah. When Pilate, upon hearing him accused by men of the highest standing among us, had condemned him to be crucified, those who had in the first place come to love him did not give up their affection for him. On the third day he appeared to them restored to life, for the prophets of God prophesied these and countless other marvelous things about him. And the tribe of the Christians, so called after him, has still to this day not disappeared.[20]

At first glance, these complimentary references to Jesus and his followers by a non-Christian historian appear to legitimize claims made by his disciples. However, it is now generally accepted that the passage was tampered with by over-zealous Christian copyists, eager to boost the faith. Josephus was a former Jewish military commander in Galilee at the time of a Jewish revolt against Roman rule, who later changed his colours, sided with Rome, and then lived under the patronage of the Emperor Vespasian. One would expect Josephus to view the budding Christianity as just another vexatious sect, just as the Romans did. That categorical reference to Jesus as "the Messiah," it is argued, could only have been written by someone who accepted him as such, which Josephus did not.

How, then, did the original passage read? While it's impossible to say with certainty, professor of Classical Civilization Michael Arnheim suggests that Josephus' description of James, found elsewhere in his book as the brother of "Jesus, the so-called Christ,"[21] may provide a clue. Arnheim says it was only this fleeting and negative reference to Jesus by Josephus that was known to Origen (ca. 185-254), one of those early church scholars and theologians who became known as a church father.[22]

Origen is regarded as early Christianity's greatest theological mind. He referred to this brief reference on several occasions, but never mentioned the longer reference. This suggests that either it had not yet been inserted into Josephus' text or else was passed over by Origen as unauthentic. It leads Arnheim and other scholars to conclude that some of the non-Christian references to Jesus were "clearly doctored by Christian copyists in order to give Jesus a more favorable non-Christian press."[23]

Origen himself appears to have been aware that the monks in the draughty scriptoria, labouring in the light of flickering candles, did make mistakes—deliberately or otherwise—as they copied the texts. He complained that "the differences among the manuscripts have become great, either through the negligence of some copyists or through the perversity of others; they either neglect to check over what they have transcribed, or, in the process of checking, they lengthen or shorten as they please."

There are other rather vague references in non-Christian literature that may, or may not, point to Jesus. For instance, the Roman historian Suetonius (ca. A.D. 70–160) wrote that the emperor Claudius expelled the Jews from Rome, because they had caused a disturbance "incited by Chrestus (sic)."[24] It is an open question among scholars as to whether or not this is a reference to Christianity.

Most scholars agree the only other non-Christian reference worthy of note is a passage from the *Annals*, written about A.D. 115, by the Roman historian Tacitus (ca. A.D. 55–117). It is far from complimentary, echoing the Romans' disdain for Christianity. In his report on the burning of Rome in Nero's time (A.D. 64), Tacitus wrote: "Christus had been executed in Tiberius' reign by the governor of Judea, Pontius Pilatus. But in spite of this temporary setback the deadly superstition had broken out afresh, not only in Judea (where the mischief had started) but even in Rome. All degraded and shameful practices collect and flourish in the capital."[25]

And then there are the references to Jesus in the Talmud—the major work of Rabbinic law and lore—which received its final editing during the fifth century A.D. It tells us that "Jesus the Nazarene" practiced magic, led Israel astray, and was hanged on the eve of the Passover. There are other references to Jesus in the Talmud suggesting that Jesus was the result of an illegitimate union between his mother and a Roman soldier.

In his book *Jesus of Nazareth*, Jewish scholar Joseph Klausner writes that the story of Jesus' illegitimacy was going the rounds in the later half of the first century, when it was told to Origen by the "heathen Celsus." However, Klausner cautions that the very few references to Jesus in the Talmud are of little historical worth because they were intended to vilify and demean Jesus, the leader of the hated

Christians. In fact, Klausner argues that such references are late interpolations inserted in the Talmud in the Middle Ages.[26]

Given the paucity of historical evidence, is it possible, as some claim, that the man we know as Jesus of Nazareth never lived? That the Bible is indeed a work of fiction? That Christianity is a gigantic fraud? British philosopher Bertrand Russell suggested that historically it is quite doubtful that Jesus ever existed at all, and if he did, we do not know anything about him. Russell, an unwavering free-thinker who nevertheless had high praise for some of Jesus' maxims, argued that if Jesus did indeed exist his message was of an imminent second coming that made all ordinary mundane affairs irrelevant. The expectation of the imminent end of the world was very much alive in the time of Russell, whose dry wit recalled a parson who "frightened his congregation terribly by telling them that the second coming was very imminent indeed, but they were much consoled when they found that he was planting trees in his garden."[27]

History may not tell us much about Jesus, the Gospels may well be full of inconsistencies, and scholars may argue about what Jesus said, or did. However, there appears to be general agreement that Jesus, or someone like him, did exist; that he was just too gigantic a figure to have been invented.

While there are, as New Testament scholar R. Joseph Hoffman notes, some scholars who would consider it extravagant even to conclude that Jesus lived and died in Judea during the Roman occupation, Christian and non-Christian sources commonly agree that he did live and die during that era. Beyond this, Hoffman says, almost no aspect of Jesus' life is indisputable: "We cannot be certain whether he was 'crucified under Pontius Pilate,' as the Gospels grudgingly acknowledge, or was stoned as a heretic by his fellow Jews, as the Talmud wants to suggest."[28]

Only a lunatic fringe has ever thought that Jesus did not exist at all, says theologian Bernard McGinn.[29] He argues that there is no good reason to doubt that Jesus was active at the beginning of the third decade of the first century; that his preaching centred on announcing the kingdom or the reign of God; and that he died by crucifixion in Jerusalem. While New Testament scholars agree that few, if any, passages in the Gospels give the very words of Jesus, "almost all are willing to identify some passages that reflect, in more or less accurate fashion, his actual preaching." The difficulty is finding two biblical scholars who completely agree on what these passages are.

Archaeologist John Romer concurs there can be little doubt that Jesus lived, even though, for more than a century now, many convinced Christian scholars have held that nothing at all remains of this man Jesus or of his humble life, that he has become a mythic, literary figure. This, he says, does not mean that according to the normal criteria of historians Jesus may be said not to have existed.

Consider, as Romer does, the all-conquering Alexander the Great who, in his short life, spread his kingdom and Greek culture from the eastern Mediterranean to the Indus River. Proclaimed a god during his lifetime, his exploits spawned legends and myths after his death in 323 B.C. Like Jesus, Alexander put his own distinctive stamp on history.

But unlike the warrior-king, Jesus was a humble man. As Romer points out, there are no coins stamped with his likeness, no contemporary inscriptions telling of his passing. And why should there be? When archaeologists excavated Capernaum on the shore of Lake Galilee, said to be the base of Jesus' ministry, they found no names of villagers inscribed there. "Such humble people rarely leave records of their passing," Romer says.

> It is unreasonable to expect to find contemporary records of Jesus or Peter in such a place. Yet from a village by this lake and from the words of the Gospels came such an energy, such an effect, that unless the whole movement was a confidence trick of unparalleled dimensions, it is more reasonable to assume that a man called Jesus really lived in Palestine during the Roman Governorate.[30]

Like most New Testament scholars, Steve Humphries-Brooks accepts that there are some basic historical facts about Jesus: he was a first-century Palestinian Jew who preached and taught in the highlands of Galilee, who went down to Jerusalem, got into trouble with both the religious and the Roman authorities, and ended up on the cross. "There's no big fuss about that in the scholarly community," says Humphries-Brooks. "The fuss starts when you try to reconstruct the actual teachings of Jesus, the range of his ideology, his possible motivations, his ministry and how he was perceived by his contemporaries."[31]

And what a lot of fuss it has stirred up, starting a scant few years after Jesus' death. Christianity swept through the world, but, as Loyola University theologian John White argues, it did not spring fully mature and pristine, like the mythical Athena, direct from the head of God. White takes issue with those who argue that Christianity was somehow virtually untouched by pagan influence. As he puts it, Christianity arose out of Judaism, and Jews were "subject to the same cultural forces that were influencing paganism. Everyone was breathing the same cultural air. Even Moses' law was being defined more universally and in a less racially specific way in Paul's time."[32]

So it is argued that Christianity, which began as a Jewish messianic sect (as much a part of Judaism as any other movement that grew up within it), was gradually usurped by Greeks and Romans and remodelled into a religion with such non-Jewish features as a saviour and afterlife salvation. This new religion, based on the teachings of a man who was born, lived, and died a Jew, was thrust into a cauldron of diverse and competing philosophical ideas. Having been transformed by his followers from an executed criminal into a divine figure, the resurrected Jesus, suggests the German philosopher Manfred Barthel, "was sent abroad to strange peoples to compete with their mythical savior gods."[33]

And, we must note, it was a world replete with gods and other mythical figures. Divinity was not unique, and many laid claim to it.

There was nothing extraordinary about being of both divine and human parentage. The mother of Augustus, the Caesar when Jesus was born, is said to have fallen asleep in the temple when Apollo appeared and impregnated her; and legend has it that the ancient Mesopotamian god Tammuz was born of a virgin, died with a wound in his abdomen, and rose from the dead from his rock tomb after three days.

"To announce in the Roman world that 'we've got another guy who is divine' would get you a big yawn, unlike in our world where it might get you media attention," says Dominic Crossan. "The argument of Celsus [ca. A.D. 178], the first pagan to read the Christian doctrines, was not that these things did not happen but that God would not have had anything to do with a peasant woman."[34]

Nevertheless, the word went forth that there was a new saviour God, born of a virgin and "the Holy Spirit," who had come to replace the old pantheon of the gods. Early Christian missionaries, fanning out through the Roman Empire, brought this new religion into cities full of idols, arguing that their God was not made of "gold, or silver or stone, an image formed by the art and imagination of mortals" (Acts 17:29).

This proved to be a potent argument. Despite bitter internal conflicts and periods of persecution, the new religion was to triumph. Like a gentle tide, it spread through the Roman Empire until it became a raging flood in the fifth century, toppling the old pagan society and replacing it with a new order.

By the beginning of the fifth century, Christian mobs were mutilating statues of pagan gods, and the church's foremost theologian, Augustine (A.D. 354-430), was rejoicing that the "whole world has become a choir praising Christ." By the end of the fifth century, the Christian church was powerful enough to demand that its followers divest themselves of any lingering attachment to the old pagan ways. In A.D. 490, the bishop of Rome warned the faithful that they should either celebrate the ancient festivities of Lupercalia as their pagan ancestors did, or acknowledge that it was "superstitious and vain and manifestly incompatible with the profession of Christianity."

The old gods gradually faded from view. Art historian John Langeloth states that "their worship continued in hiding in restricted and clandestine circles, but their existence was ever more spectral. Their health had depended on the upkeep of their statues, and as these crumbled their influence waned. The images of Christ had put them all to rout."[35]

Ironically, it was a pagan and superstitious emperor who helped replace the old idols with the new God of Christianity.

The Idols Fall 3

Measuring eight feet from its neck to the top of its skull, the fourth-century marble head of Constantine the Great in Rome's Capitoline Museums once topped a colossal statue of the mighty Roman emperor. The head's immodest size, those "huge, radiant eyes, the massive, immobile features,"[1] speak of supreme confidence, raw strength, dogged determination and imperial power. In sharp contrast, the life-size marble statue of Constantine in a Vatican antechamber depicts a man dazzled by a higher power. Commissioned by Pope Innocent X in the early seventeenth century, it was frozen in time by the master of baroque art, Gianlorenzo Bernini. It shows a cut-down-to-size Constantine astride a rearing horse, gazing in awe at a sign in the heavens.

The year is A.D. 312, and Constantine is at war with Maxentius, his rival for mastery of the western Roman Empire. Christianity is still a scorned, ridiculed, and often persecuted minority movement, subject to the whim of whoever is in power.

Tradition has it that prior to a decisive battle with the forces of his rival, Constantine had a vision that helped pave the way to the emperor's throne. Years after Constantine's death, the scholar-bishop Eusebius (A.D. 260–340), the "father of church history" and the emperor's long-time aide and confidant, recorded what he said the emperor had told him about that vision:

> He said that with his own eyes ... while the day was already fading, he had seen a shining cross in the sky more brilliant than the sun, accompanied by the words *In Hoc Signo Vinces*—By this sign, thou shalt conquer. He remained stunned by the vision, and so did all the army following him in the expedition, which had also seen the miracle."[2]

Adopting the cross as his army's emblem, and ordering his soldiers to paint Christian monograms on their shields, Constantine routed Maxentius' forces at the battle of Milvian Bridge, outside Rome. Constantine was on his way to supreme power, and he brought Christianity along with him.

Historian Robin Lane Fox notes that, like so many other warriors from Homer's poem onwards, Constantine was empowered by a heavenly sign. He was apparently prone to seeing visions, having earlier experienced a vision of Apollo in a temple in Gaul. But he was of an age when visions were a known phenomenon, and with the proper offering, the gods were expected to intervene in human affairs. This we can say: Constantine's vision changed the course of human history.[3]

A year after the battle of Milvian Bridge, the two emperors, Constantine in the west and his fellow pagan Licinius in the east, issued the Edict of Milan. This edict tolerated all cults, including Christianity, which allowed the Christians to come out of hiding into the full rights of citizenship. Three hundred years after its birth, having survived derision, odium, persecution, and its own internal conflicts, Christianity now occupied an equal, even a favoured, position among the other religions of the empire.

The emperor's conversion and subsequent actions marked "another great turning point in the interaction of the Church with history," says University of Notre Dame theologian Richard P. McBrien. The new emperor pursued a vigorous campaign against pagan practices whilst lavishing money and monuments upon the Christian church. Roman law was modified to accommodate Christian values, and the clergy were accorded privileged status. For some historians, says McBrien, this signalled the beginning of a sort of "Caesar is Pope" era, with the church utterly dependent upon the state, and forced eventually to subordinate its spiritual interests to political considerations. It is also true that the conversion of Constantine "provided the Church with extraordinary opportunities for proclaiming the Gospel to all nations and for bringing necessary order into doctrinal and liturgical life. It also allowed the Church to be less defensive about pagan culture, to learn from it and to be enriched by it."[4] But, for some time, Christianity remained one faith among many.

Historians have cast a cold eye on Constantine's commitment to Christianity. They have painted him as a political opportunist who supported Christianity because it proved itself useful in winning the battle of Milvian Bridge. Eusebius' account of an entire army stunned by a vision is always with us, but, as historian John Romer points out, the coins struck in celebration of this victory were not dedicated to the God of Jesus Christ but to the Roman legion's perennial favourite, Sol Invictus.[5]

Constantine was certainly not the prototype of a model Christian leader, nor was he the last to hack his way to power with a bloody sword to satisfy his "cold and terrible lust for power." Historians have suggested that the emperor's policy of uniting the various feuding Christian factions was directed more towards expanding the empire than the salvation of his soul. His was a death-bed baptism, literally. Tradition tells us that he was baptized in A.D. 337 by his long-time adviser, Eusebius.

Whatever his motives, it is true that between his defeat of Maxentius and his death, Constantine advanced Christianity everywhere on the map of the so-called known world. For ardent and influential churchmen such as Eusebius, Christianity and the Roman Empire were made for each other. The Emperor Augustus had united the "world" under Roman rule, Christ under God's, and Constantine welded together the two unities. "Church and empire were fused into a single entity: The Empire was an image of a heavenly kingdom, its boundaries the limits of Christiandom, the emperor, the representative of divine authority in the world."[6] Heresy became akin to treason. The mighty Roman Empire, which three centuries before had barely noticed the crucifixion in a remote outpost of an insignificant trouble-maker called Jesus, had now co-opted him to help bind the empire together. In turn, the Christian church was to adopt much of the empire's administrative structure and imperial trappings of power as it spread its message to the far corners of the known world.

That said, it must be kept in mind that Christian expansion had begun not long after Jesus' death. Only twenty years after the crucifixion, the Christian church was "well-established and beginning to grow into a highly complex organization with rules and rituals more intricate and elaborate than anything that Jesus teaches in the Gospels."[7]

Playing a starring role in the unfolding drama of a nascent church struggling to establish and define itself was the indomitable Apostle Paul. The cosmopolitan Paul—a balding, bow-legged man by some accounts—was a Roman citizen from Tarsus, a typical, cosmopolitan Hellenistic city influenced by Greek culture, which offered a variety of religious options. Paul was also a devout Jew who studied under the much revered scholar Rabbi Gamaliel (Cf. Acts 22:3).

The New Testament tells us in graphic detail that Paul, on his way to Damascus to persecute Jesus' followers, was stunned by a flash of light from heaven and heard a voice asking, "Saul, Saul, why do you persecute me?" In turn, Paul asked who was speaking and was told it was Jesus. This experience had such a profound affect on Paul that he changed his allegiance from the Torah to Christ. In taking to his new faith with a convert's zeal, Paul did much to advance Christianity outside Palestine.

Providentially, the letters Paul wrote to various Christian communities as he moved around the Mediterranean give us some colourful insights into how the early Christian church functioned. These letters, penned probably between A.D. 50 to 60, are the earliest preserved Christian texts we have and are included in the New Testament with the Gospels of Matthew, Mark, Luke, and John. Paul offers little in the way of details of Jesus' life, but his letters profoundly influenced the development of the new Christian church.

Although Luke in his Acts of the Apostles narrates Paul's conversion and travels, he and the three other Gospel writers are silent about the Apostle's informative letters. These letters show a far from untroubled early Christian church, and they deal firmly and frankly with quarrels and unseemly behaviour among early followers of Jesus. In the city of Corinth, for instance, various factions boasted of their special relationship with those who baptized them, thus setting themselves apart from other Christians. Paul waded into the conflict, appealing to the unity of all baptized Christians in Christ.

In addition, the young church was harassed by Jews who objected to Paul's preaching a new interpretation of their faith in their synagogues. One of the major problems was the conflict between two fundamentally different visions of Christianity, Jewish and Gentile. Headed by Jesus' brother James, many early followers wanted to keep what was essentially a form of Judaism, with all Jewish rituals intact. Paul's letter to the churches in Galatia in Asia Minor, written in the early 50s, is directed against followers of James who are pressuring the Galatian Christians to accept circumcision: "For before certain men came from James, he [Peter] ate with the Gentiles: but when they came he drew back and separated himself, fearing the circumcision party" (Gal. 2:12). In response, Paul holds fast to faith in Jesus Christ as the only element necessary for one to be declared righteous before God.

Paul and others viewed Christianity as a worldwide movement to be taken out of Palestine and outside the Jewish community. His

45

vision triumphed, and the Jerusalem Church, those closest to the historical Jesus, hated him for it. The animosity was so strong that the second-century Jewish-Christian document *Preaching of Peter* (*Kerygmata Petrou*) even depicts Paul as Simon Magnus, the Magician, who tried to buy magical powers from Peter. The *Kerygmata* contains fictitious lectures and debates of Peter, as well as an unauthentic letter of Peter to James. Many scholars contend that the *Kerygmata* contains traditions that go back as far as the early Catholic Church and reflects the growing rift between Jewish Christianity and Gentile Christianity. James is portrayed as the unquestioned authority of Jewish Christianity and Peter is the representative of a law-abiding Christian mission to the Gentiles who refutes Simon Magnus and his Pauline teaching.[8]

If the young church communities were to survive and carry out what they believed to be Jesus' mission, rudimentary organizational structures were needed, as well as some common standards and practices. Externally, the church had to define itself vis-à-vis its parent religion, Judaism, says historian Steve Mason. Although some groups within the church remained fully within Judaism, as is clear from Paul's letter to the Galatians and from the evidence of later Jewish-Christian groups such as the Ebionites, others broke with it entirely.

The appeal of Christianity to the pagan Gentile masses should not be underestimated. Paul hints at Christianity's drawing power among the lower classes in his letter to the Corinthians, where he gives a social profile of the community. He writes, "Not many of you were wise according to worldly standards, not many were powerful, not many were of noble birth" (1 Cor. 1:26). This sudden influx of non-Jews, together with the general unwillingness of Jews to accept Jesus as the Messiah, created major difficulties and left some Jewish Christian groups clinging to their ancient law and customs.

The first-generation church had to adapt itself to the failure of the Jewish mission, the relative success of the Gentile mission, and the hostility of the Romans. It also had to deal with the delay of Jesus' return and adjust its preaching accordingly.[9] By the time the evangelist Luke wrote the Acts of the Apostles, such adaptations were well underway. As Luke narrates it in Acts, when Jesus ascended into heaven an angel announced to the apostles that, at an unspecified time in the future, they would see Christ coming from heaven, just as they saw him ascend into heaven (1:11). The final chapter of Acts depicts the Jews as a nation that has rejected Jesus. Therefore God's salvation has been passed over to the Gentiles (28:26-30).

Was Paul from the outset simply obeying Christ's command to preach to all nations when he proclaimed the new religion to the Gentiles? Or did the rejection of the Christian message by most Jews force Paul to look for more fertile ground? If Jews would not accept Jesus as the Messiah, then those who did accept him would be received as the true chosen people.

Paul's decision to go out to the Gentiles and convert them to faith in Christ is viewed as one of the decisive points in the history of first-century Christianity. Some scholars go so far as to argue that, had he not done so, it is most unlikely that Christianity would have come into existence at all—the belief that Jesus was the promised Messiah could well have been absorbed by the Judaism of the day, thus negating the need for a new religion. Consider the case of the modern-day Lubavitch movement, followers of Rabbi Menachem Schneerson, who died in 1994. Many Lubavitchers believe that the Russian-born, Brooklyn-based rabbi who never visited Israel is the long awaited Messiah and eagerly await his return to earth. Although mainstream Jews generally tend to view the movement as an embarrassing anachronism, it is still considered part of the Jewish family.

Of course, Christ's followers with their "good news" message were on the move before Paul. Indeed, by the time of his conversion, only a few years after Jesus' crucifixion, a number of Christian communities had already come into being—not only in Palestine but also elsewhere in Asia Minor. When Paul was being escorted to Rome while under arrest, there were church members waiting to greet him at several stops along the way. At Sidon, in modern-day Syria, the centurion guarding Paul allowed him to visit some friends. The Christian community at the Bay of Naples urged Paul to spend a week with them. When word of his arrival reached Rome, some Roman Christians travelled forty-nine kilometres south to wait for him at the "Three Taverns." Some went further, to the Forum of Appius, sixty-five kilometres south of Rome. On seeing this display of support, Paul "thanked God and took courage" (Acts 28:11-15).

Despite the Trojan efforts of his predecessors and contemporaries, it is the energetic, letter-writing Paul who stands out head and shoulders above the first generation of Christian missionaries who bore witness to the gospel "in Jerusalem, and in all Judea and Samaria, and to the ends of the earth" (Acts 1:8). By the end of Paul's life, outposts of the new faith were flourishing from Palestine north to Syria and across the northern rim of the Mediterranean through Asia Minor and Greece to Rome. The church that started off as predominantly Jewish was becoming increasingly Gentile.

Paul's contribution to the early spread of Christianity has led some scholars to argue that, while Jesus inspired and gave his name to Christianity, it was really Paul who shaped it, or was its chief architect. Although Paul's dominant role in spreading Christianity is not a matter of dispute among scholars, the full extent of his influence is. As early as 1901, the German New Testament scholar William Wrede (1859-1906) caused a stir when he maintained that Jesus did not claim to be the Messiah and that the Christian religion received its essential form largely through Paul's radical transformation of Christ's teaching.[10]

Any examination of Paul's part in the early Christian saga produces one common question: why are there are so few points of contact between Paul and the Gospel traditions about Jesus? As English theologian John Court notes in a review of the 1995 book *Paul: Follower of Jesus or Founder of Christianity?*,[11] both biblical scholars and theologians see a problem in the apparent lack of continuity between the teaching and understanding of Jesus himself as seen in the Gospels, and what Paul understood and taught in his letters. For example, Paul says Jesus was "born of woman" but does not suggest a virgin birth. Likewise Paul emphasizes the importance of the crucifixion and the resurrection, but seems uninterested in Jesus' biography. The only other explicit references to the Gospel traditions, Court says, are to the Last Supper and a few isolated themes from Jesus' teaching.[12]

The link between Paul and Gospel traditions may be thin, but scholars such as Steve Mason reject the idea that Paul "invented" Christianity, calling the idea "idiosyncratic." He argues that Paul cites established traditions in his letters to Christian communities and that we can make sense of Paul only if there were already an existing level of Christian consciousness. For example, when Paul writes to Christians in Corinth, he tells them that he is only passing on to them what he has heard about the resurrection and other events.[13]

Richard Valantasis, assistant professor of New Testament and Early Church at St. Louis University, has no doubts that Christianity originated with Jesus. He sees Jesus as a Jew in the same mould as the Jewish prophet Isaiah, who proclaimed his message to the Gentile nations. He views Jesus as a universalist, who spoke to all types of different groups, with each group interpreting him differently. So Valantasis rejects the idea that the universal message preached by Jesus was Paul's creation. Even though Paul didn't actually know him, he was typical of Jesus' early itinerant followers. And although there is no direct evidence to prove it, it is distinctly possible there were Gentile missionaries before Paul who established Christian communities outside of Palestine.[14]

Paul did preach in synagogues, but as Religion professor Elaine Pagels notes, he found his audience largely among Gentiles, most often among Gentiles attracted to Jewish congregations. Proclaiming that Jews and Gentiles, slaves and free people, men and women, could now become "one in Christ," Paul formed diverse communities where "trades people, slaves, and the groups of wealthy patrons mingled together now bound to help and support one another as they awaited the time when Christ would return in glory."[15]

Identity was the Christian crisis of the second century, says English theologian Charles Lowry in his book, *The First Theologians*; it was the most serious and the most dangerous period that the church had known. What was proposed was nothing less than the rejection and expulsion of the whole Jewish background of Christianity. Where Paul, in writing to the Romans in the middle 50s, lauded the Jews as the source of "all that was precious and distinctive in the Christian heritage," the second-century intellectuals of a "heretical" movement known as Gnosticism wanted to free Christianity from the "inferior impediments of the Old Testament."[16]

After Jewish authorities closed the Synagogue to envoys or apostles of Christ, Jewish-Christian relations turned bitter. As a consequence, the Christians saw the Jews as having wilfully turned away from the love of God in Jesus Christ. Once Christianity had shaken free from its Jewish roots, says Geoffrey Barraclough, it embarked on its missionary career, seeking to convert the pagans to the Christian faith and a Christian way of life. It may be one explanation for Christianity's survival: rejected by the Jews, its only prospective field of activity was among the Gentiles.[17]

Urged on by the belief that they were doing God's work, those early "missionaries" spread the Christian message, converting large numbers to the fold. Christianity was to survive sporadic persecutions and become a social force to be reckoned with. Internally, however, conflicting theological opinions threatened to tear small communities apart. The tendencies of "false brethren" to separate and form a church around their own beliefs is already clear in Paul's letters and elsewhere in the New Testament. Paul mentions the "false brethren" who opposed him when he went to Jerusalem with Barnabas.[18]

By the early fourth century, Christianity was laced with "heresy," bedevilled by sects, and loud with claims and counter-claims over a "true" understanding of the person of Jesus. As Leonard Levy, a contemporary historian, notes, the varieties of Christianity were probably as numerous as those of today. As well as followers of what was a loose consensus on orthodox teaching, there were followers of many fringe groups and "varieties of so-called Jewish Christians, most of whom were not Jewish but agreed with Jews on circumcision, the Sabbath, diet, and the humanity of Jesus." The real Jewish Christians, says Levy, those members of the first Jerusalem Church who were the closest to Jesus, held beliefs that by the second century were regarded by the majority as heretical and blasphemous.[19] For example, as an early Christian historian noted, the heretical group called Ebionites "affirm that the Christ was born of Joseph and Mary, and suppose Him to be mere man, and strongly maintain the Law ought to be kept in a more strictly Jewish fashion."[20]

Compounding the problem was the absence of a strong central authority that could insist on its version of correct teaching. Crucial to this was the need to agree on which biblical texts were deemed to be "received" and which were to be viewed as dubious, unacceptable, heretical.

This was the situation after Constantine had forged east and west together into one Roman Empire. A divided, factious Christianity threatened the empire's hard-won unity. Not only were the disputes displeasing to heaven, they were also an impediment to success and prosperity. With this in mind, Constantine turned his attention to unifying Christianity and, in 325, he convened the Council of Nicaea, not far from modern Istanbul. This gathering of bishops was held in a great hall of the emperor's palace and was presided over by him. "Tall, slender and full of grace and majesty," he opened the proceedings "stiff with purple, gold and precious stones."[21]

The council's main concern was the Arian heresy, named after the Libyan Arius (250-336), a priest of the Egyptian city of Alexandria, famous for its intellectual as well as commercial wealth. In this city, where free-wheeling philosophical discussions were the norm,

Arius preached that God was the father—one infinite and indivis-ible—and had no equals. Consequently, he argued that the son could not be "true God." He summed up his argument with the phrase "There was once when he [the Son] was not." Although excommuni-cated and banished by a council of Egyptian and Libyan bishops, Arius found support for his teaching among some prominent church leaders, including Eusebius. As a consequence, the controversy swirl-ing around the true divinity of Christ was as divisive as the one that surrounded Paul's mission to the Gentiles almost three centuries ear-lier. For the unity of the church—and the empire—it had to be set-tled.[22]

Although the Council of Nicaea has been described as the first worldwide gathering of bishops in history, it was far from representa-tive of the whole church. Of approximately eighteen hundred bish-ops invited to attend at the emperor's expense, only three hundred or so took up his invitation and almost all of them were from the east. The Latin west was represented by only three or four bishops, and Pope Sylvester delegated two Roman priests to attend in his place. After several weeks of debate, the council arrived at a resolution that would remain at the core of Christian doctrine; a declaration of faith, a statement of Christian belief, known to later centuries as the Nicene Creed, which affirmed that the Son is equal in status to the Father. Only two bishops refused to accept the Creed. They and Arius were sent into exile. Constantine decreed that those caught with Arian books would be treated as criminals and suffer capital punishment; beliefs were truly a matter of life and death.[23]

Despite Constantine's draconian decree, the Arian argument, now branded heresy, continued to be a painful thorn in Christian teach-ing. The fierce debate over Jesus' nature raged for decades. It was an issue of such intense public preoccupation that Gregory of Nyssa (ca. 330-395), the champion of Nicene orthodoxy, complained that he could not buy a loaf of bread or get his hair cut without people start-ing a discussion on how the Son shared the Father's nature.[24]

By 350, it was the Arians who were triumphant. After Constantine's death, the united empire was split among his three sons. One of his sons, Constantius II, reunited east and west under the Arian banner and several church councils endorsed Arian views, denouncing what happened at Nicaea as blasphemous.[25] It wasn't until A.D. 381 at the First Council of Constantinople—convened by the Emperor Theodosius the Great, who formally declared Christianity to be the empire's state religion—that the orthodoxy of Nicaea was to triumph.

However, the theological infighting over Jesus' nature continued. In 431, the Council of Ephesus met to respond to unorthodox teachings that there were two separate persons in Christ, one divine and the other human, as opposed to the orthodox teaching that Christ was one divine person. The unorthodox view was espoused by the monk Nestorius, who became Patriarch of Constantinople and was later deposed and banished to upper Egypt, where he died. Eastern bishops who refused to accept the orthodox formula separated to form the Nestorian Church, which became active in missionary work and established Christian settlements in Arabia, India, and as far away as China. However, the issue was far from settled and, in 451, the Council of Chalcedon—said to be the most important church council after Nicaea—reaffirmed in clear terms the church's scriptural and traditional faith in the unity (one person) and the distinction (two natures) in Jesus Christ. This formula, which was again reaffirmed by the Third Council of Constantinople in 681, has continued for fifteen centuries.

All this complex theological discussion may well have confounded the man in the barber shop. It appears that even pontiffs had difficulty sorting out the theological soundness of one position over another. The "truth" of the words could be elusive. When the Third Council of Constantinople condemned as heretical the view that Christ had "one will," which led inevitably to the conclusion that he had "one nature," it also chastised the deceased Pope Honorius who, years earlier, had approved the heresy.[26]

The war of words generated by different interpretations of church doctrine must have kept the theologians happy. It appears that some of them could spend years, even a lifetime, in arcane theological debate. Take, for example, the *filioque* clause—a Latin term, meaning "and the son"—which was added to the Nicene Creed to counter the Arian heresy. The idea that the Holy Spirit proceeds from the Father and the Son was a subject of theological disagreement between Christian theologians as early as the fourth century and the cause of division by the ninth century. Eastern theologians who insisted there must be a single source of divinity in God refused to approve the inclusion of the *filioque* clause into the Creed, believing it to be not only an illegitimate addition but a grave theological error. The dispute came to a head in 1054 when the Roman church branded patriarchs of the east as heretics, laying a bull of excommunication on the altar in Constantinople's Hagia Sophia. Excommunications and anathemae flew back and forth. The ensuing schism continues today, and the *filioque* clause remains a barrier between Roman and Orthodox Catholics.[27]

The disputes that focussed on the nature of Jesus and on the Trinity were complicated to no end by the issue of language. They were in part, says systematic theologian Ovey Mohammed, disputes between Greek-speaking Christians and Oriental Christians who, though using Greek for theological discussions, had Syrian, Armenian, or Coptic for their mother tongue. The existence of Latin-speaking Christians further complicated the matter.

So, as Ovey Mohammed points out, the doctrines finally hammered out by the church represent a compromise between Greek-speaking and Latin-speaking Christians, leaving Oriental Christians out in the cold, so to speak. The agreed upon formulations were Western and attempts to impose them on people in the Middle East resulted in friction, which festers to this day.[28]

Christendom owes another debt of gratitude to Constantine: six years after the Council of Nicaea arrived at a resolution concerning the nature of Christ, the emperor ordered his secretary Eusebius to arrange the production of fifty Bibles. In an age when copying manuscripts was a long and laborious task, carried out by scribes with quill pens, this was no small venture. The Bibles were to be written on fine parchment, for use in the churches of Constantinople, the new Christian capital of the empire. The emperor paid all expenses. He also provided two carriages to assure the swift shipment of the completed copies for his inspection.

The emperor was paying the piper and so was calling the tune. And there was nobody around brave enough, or foolish enough, to tell him that the question of what books should be in the canon, and what books should be left out, was still unresolved.[29] Some scholars suggest that if there was a moment in history when the church was forced to decide the issue of which books would make up the New Testament—when the New Testament canon was settled for all practical purposes—this was it.

What is Truth? 4

T he oldest known New Testament record is a snippet of papyrus no bigger than a human hand. It was discovered in a Cairo shop in 1920, and was dated by its style of handwriting to about A.D. 130. This priceless flake of papyrus contains details of Jesus' last days as recorded by the Gospel writer John. On one side of the fragment are snatches of the trial of Jesus before the Jewish Council. Recorded on the other side is Pilate's response to Jesus' statement that everyone who belonged to the truth listened to his voice.

"What is truth?" Pilate asked.

That question elicits various responses when applied to the Bible, depending on who is interpreting the text. Like the search for the historical Jesus, people tend to find what they are looking for. William Blake, the great early nineteenth-century English poet-mystic, made this point with simple whimsy:

> The Vision of Christ that thou dost see
> Is my vision's greatest enemy:
> Thine has a great hook nose like thine,
> Mine has a snub nose like to mine....
> Both read the Bible day and night,
> But thou read'st black where I read white.[1]

The books in the Bible (from the medieval Latin *biblia*) were written during a period from a thousand years before Christ to about a hundred years after his death. It is divided into the Old Testament, a collection of thirty-nine books from the Jewish tradition, and the New Testament, comprising twenty-seven books that primarily deal with Jesus' life and mission. It has been lauded as the "Book of books, the storehouse and magazine of life and comfort." It has also been condemned "as one of the most contemptible and brutalizing books ever penned," a history of lust, sodomies, slaughter, and depravity. It has been used to justify slavery, war, and the oppression of women. It has also been used to support a new order, where Jew and Greek, slave and free, male and female are one in Christ Jesus.

For many, the Bible, both the Old and New Testament, is both inspirational and historical. At times, this has led to over-zealous claims. For example, using the Bible as his source and, with "a truly Renaissance combination of enthusiasm, industry and biblical scholarship," the nineteenth-century Bishop James Ussher of Armagh, Ireland, calculated that God created the heavens and the earth at precisely noon on Sunday, October 23, in the year 4004 B.C. Still more surprising, that date was challenged by the distinguished French Jesuit theologian Petavius, who calculated that the creation had actually occurred twenty-one years later on Monday, October 26.[2]

As has been noted, what are known as the four canonical Gospels of Matthew, Mark, Luke, and John in the Bible's New Testament are the major source of our information about Jesus. And they do lend themselves to interpretation: there may only be one Jesus, but there is more than one Gospel. As a consequence, there is more than one interpretation. And, as Dominic Crossan points out, the fact that these four do not represent all the early gospels available, or even a random sample of them, compounds the problem.

What we have, says Crossan, is a "calculated collection" known as the canonical Gospels; the set of books accepted as the authoritative standard of the church's faith and worship. As a result, these four Gospels are a "spectrum of approved interpretation forming a strong central vision that was later used to render apocryphal, hidden or censored" any other gospel that did not conform with the church's selection. Read the four Gospel narratives consecutively, from start to finish and, he suggests, you get a generally persuasive impression of unity, harmony, and agreement. Put the four books beside one another, focus on a particular passage in one of the Gospels and compare it with what is in the others, and it is "disagreement rather than agreement that strikes you most forcibly."

Most scholars, including many conservatives, recognize that the four "biographies" of Jesus show marked disagreement. Just what, for example, were the last words of Jesus before his death? How does Jesus die? asks DePaul University professor Jeffrey Carlson. With serene confidence as in Luke: "Father, into your hands I commend my spirit"? Or abandoned and in despair as in Matthew and Mark: "My God, My God, why have you forsaken me"? Carlson notes other inconsistencies. Was Jesus born in a manger? Yes, but only in Luke. Were there wise men following a star? Yes, but only in Matthew. John and Mark don't even mention Jesus' birth, an event most Christians would consider to be one of history's most important dates.[3]

Is the Bible true? Theologian William Placher says that whenever there is a really intense fight among American Protestants, sooner or later it seems to turn into an argument over the truth of scripture. At one extreme, some dismiss any appeal to the Bible out of hand and consider "authority" a dirty word. Others, he says, confidently assert that only their literalistic interpretations really count in assessing the Bible's veracity. And there are many like Placher himself, "wandering around confused in the middle, wanting to believe in the Bible, not thinking of ourselves as biblical literalists, but unsure how to characterize our position."

Much of the "notorious malaise of mainstream Protestantism," Placher suggests, derives from a perception that to the question, "Is the Bible true?" the moderate answer is, "Well, sort of...," followed by either a lot of confused talk or an embarrassed silence."[4]

And yet, it is from early Bible lessons as well as from Sunday school classes, from stained glass windows, pious pictures in first-grade catechisms, and other sources that Christians inherit their image of Jesus. And very often, says Christian writer Philip Yancey, the image is that of a "Mr. Rogers with a beard." Some never let go of that image. Others, like Yancey, have been forced to make a dramatic reassessment.

The Sunday school portrayals of Jesus that Yancey carried with him to Bible College showed Jesus wearing a moustache and a beard, and both facial adornments were considered inappropriate and strictly banned from the college. Ironically, it took the Marxist Italian Pier Paola Pasolini's movie, *The Gospel According to St. Matthew*, to help Yancey make a "disturbing re-evaluation" of Jesus' physical appearance. "I could not dodge the fact that the words in Pasolini's film were taken entirely from Matthew's Gospel," he says, "yet their message clearly did not fit my prior conception of Jesus." Despite having to jettison his earlier image of Jesus, he remains a conservative Christian who believes the Gospels possess a "self-authenticating authority." He has read Dominic Crossan and other liberal scholars and does not consider their conclusions a threat to his faith: "I really don't think that the Jesus portrayed in the Gospels could have been made up."[5]

For Yancey and millions of other Christians, the Bible is a source of inspiration, a moral and ethical handbook. Translated into almost all the world's languages, it has been a long-time best-seller—for 100,000 weeks, the Canadian Bible Society likes to boast, with a touch of Madison Avenue advertising license. But just how many read it is another question. In late 1995, the British Bible Society revealed that nearly two-thirds of regular churchgoers do not read the Bible regularly and that 15 percent have never read anything from the Bible.[6] A 1993 Decima Research Report conducted for the Canadian Bible Society showed similar results. In an effort to attract readers, the American Bible Society published a contemporary English version of the Bible aimed at those with a 5.4 Grade reading level or less. This Bible, the Society boasts, is as easy to read as the daily newspaper, as well as being a faithful translation of "God's word."

In any discussion about the origin of the New Testament—that collection of early church writings comprising Paul's letters, the Gospels of Matthew, Mark, Luke, and John, and twenty-two other books— several things must be noted. Although the New Testament was written in Greek, the language that Jesus and his disciples spoke was Aramaic. Also, there is no autograph copy of any single New Testament book, which is hardly surprising given the highly perishable nature of the material on which they were written. What we do have are five thousand copies or fragments. However, no two copies agree in every detail, and again this is hardly surprising. Manuscripts were hand-copied and, as a consequence, subject to the inevitability of human error as well as a scribe's whim.

We know that Paul authored the letters. What we don't know is who wrote the Gospels, because anonymous works in antiquity were often attributed to prominent persons. Take the Gospel of Matthew as an example. Based on a reference in this Gospel to a "scribe trained for the kingdom of heaven," there is specuation that it was composed by an unknown Greek-speaking Jewish Christian who was probably a scribe. In the second century, the Gospel was attributed to Matthew, one of Jesus' twelve disciples, to give it authority.

Early tradition had it that Mark's Gospel was written by a companion of Peter. Yet nowhere in this Gospel is its author identified, so the authorship of Mark "remains an enigma, perhaps by the author's design." Likewise, early tradition attributes Luke's Gospel to a companion of Paul, whom he greeted as the "beloved physician" and "fellow co-worker" (Col. 4:14; Phil. 24). Yet here again the name Luke never appears in the Gospel. John's Gospel is attributed to the disciple "whom Jesus loved," but the Gospel itself does not make this identification and neither mentions John nor names its author.[7]

It must also be noted that in the time of Jesus and in the early years of the church, the "Bible" was what we call the Old Testament. When Paul dictated his letters to the early Christian communities in Asia Minor, the "Gospels" as we know them had yet to be written. Paul could not have known he was writing "scripture," or that his letters would end up in a best-selling book with the great writings of the Jewish prophets and the Christian Gospels.

As historian Steve Mason points out, the early church was content to maintain the Jewish Bible as its own, with Jesus' teachings and the Apostles' writings as an interpretive key well into the second century. However, when Christianity and Judaism began to drift apart, because of the mission to the Gentiles and the expulsion of Christians from Jewish communities, Christianity began to "emphasize its distinctive writings."[8]

The first stage in the long process that produced the New Testament was the creation of early Christian documents from the oral transmissions of the Christian message. Not everyone was enthusiastic about the written word. For instance, Papias, the second-century Bishop of Hieropolis in Phrygea, Asia Minor, recalled that when anyone came along who had been a follower of the Apostles, he would "inquire about the Apostles' discourses: what was said by Andrew, or by Peter, or by Philip, Thomas or James.... It did not seem to me that I could get as much profit from the contents of books as from a living and abiding voice."[9] However, as the first generation of eyewitnesses died out, the writings gained prominence and were later put together in collections of varying texts. Together with Paul's letters, which were exchanged and collected from an early date, the Gospels became the "scriptures" most used by the early church. But they were not the only writings making the rounds of the early Christian communities.

Biblical scholar Robert Funk notes that a culture that lives by the oral word treats sources and wording with much more liberty than those of us accustomed to print culture and copyright laws: "Plagiarism and copyright were unknown concepts in the ancient world.

Sages attracted wise words the way a magnet attracts iron fillings,"[10] which explains the emergence of a plethora of diverse writings about Jesus in early Christianity.

The evangelist Luke, writing in the late eighties of the first century A.D., opens his Gospel by informing readers that many before him had undertaken to set down "an orderly account" of the events. The reference to "orderly account" may also suggest that Luke was aware of a wide variety of conflicting narratives (1:1-4). A century after Luke, Irenaeus, the bishop of Lyons (ca. 130–200), complained of "an unspeakable number of apocryphal and spurious writings, which they themselves [heretics] had forged, to bewilder the mind of the foolish." Later, the third-century Origen lamented that while the church possessed four Gospels, heresy possessed a great many. So the conviction grew that what was needed was an authoritative, universally accepted holy book to respond to the clamour and counterclaims of growing "heretical" movements such as Gnosticism—a complex, multi-faceted religious belief system. Originating in pagan circles, Gnosticism's Christian expression flowered in the second century. Among other things, Gnostics denied Jesus' full humanity.

Out of a desire to create some order in what must have been a turbulent sea was born the writings we know as the New Testament— the canon, from the Greek *norm* or *rule*, the standard by which things can be measured. If those early Christians, prompted by an urgent need to respond to attacks from "heretical" sects, prayed for the speedy production of such a book, their prayers remained unanswered. It did not appear overnight. It was, in fact, to be a complex, bewildering, and meandering endeavour. Rather than being an "edifice erected miraculously at a single stroke," it was the result of a human and historical process that took centuries.[11]

"Conservatives would like to think that the formation of the New Testament canon was a simple, rapid process orchestrated by God and no one else," says John Meier. "On the conservative Protestant side, one hears talk of the canon imposing itself upon the Church.

On the conservative Catholic side there is a hazy idea that some council and/or Pope issued a dogmatic definition early on that settled the whole matter."[12]

We know that the process of producing one unified book was hastened by the early church's response to a wealthy ship owner, a bishop's son named Marcion (d. ca. 160). He preached a Christianity that denied Jesus' connections with Jews and with the Old Testament and argued that all Jewish connections with God had been inspired by the devil and elaborated by sinful men. Like other Christians of his era, Marcion knew the authoritative Christian scripture—in his time, the Old Testament—and the still undefined and mostly oral traditions of the apostles and early writings, which transmitted the words and deeds of Jesus. Marcion proposed that the church reject the Jewish scriptures and embrace a new canon of its own, a non-Jewish Bible containing just one Gospel, Luke, and one Apostle, Paul.[13]

Marcion has been described as "the first Protestant " because of his radical interpretation of Paul's distinction between law and gospel. Some early church authorities were less charitable, calling him the arch heretic and the devil's first born. They met Marcion's challenge by drawing up lists of books that were approved to be read in the churches. Marcion was excommunicated—in modern terms, excluded from the life of what was an emerging Christian church.

It was Irenaeus, in the second century, who first made a case for incorporating the Gospels of Matthew, Mark, Luke, and John into the canon. That there was an urgent need for such a canon was confirmed for Irenaeus when he visited Rome and found its churches filled with all manner of sects and cells. In his book *Against the Heresies*, he "laid out the orthodoxies of the Christian Church, its faith, preaching and the books it held as sacred authority," suggesting that he wanted to make a clear statement of a faith that was "being muddied and obscured" by the claims and secrecy of many Christian sects. A decade after Marcion proposed his "heretical" canon, Irenaeus claimed that his canonical selection had long been authenticated because the writings had been used by early church fathers and the earlier generations, "those who had seen the Lord."[14] Even more dubiously, he further argued that, just as there are only four principal winds and four corners of the universe and four pillars holding up the sky, so there can be only four Gospels.[15]

Irenaeus' objective and hope, states Elaine Pagels, was the consolidation of Christian groups already threatened by persecution. The gospels he chose and endorsed "helped institutionalize the Christian movement; those he denounced as heresy did not serve the purposes of institutionalization." Some, on the contrary, urged people to seek direct access to God, unmediated by church or clergy. By the late second century, according to Pagel, bishops of the church, who called themselves orthodox, rejected all but the four canonical Gospels, denouncing all the rest, in Irenaeus' words, as "an abyss of madness and blasphemy against Christ."[16]

But even among the church's so-called orthodox faction, the issue of which books constituted the New Testament remained clouded. As Roy Hoover notes, by the time of Constantine's adviser Eusebius, there was a consensus on at least twenty-one books that were to be included. Eusebius divided the various book into three categories: acknowledged, disputed, and rejected. In his list of A.D. 325, Eusebius named twenty-one books as acknowledged, listing Revelation twice, once among the acknowledged and once among the disputed; the sincere religious search for truth has never been easy or unambiguous. Interestingly, many of the sacred writings that Eusebius excluded from his collection of orthodox books had been circulating among Christians for generations. Yet he declared that much of their content was so out of harmony with orthodoxy as to make them heretical. For this reason "they ought not even be placed among the spurious writings, but refused as altogether monstrous and impious."[17]

The first list that tallies with the contents of our current New Testament was issued by Athanasius, Bishop of Alexandria, Egypt, in 367. Within a century or two, this list was accepted as authoritative all over the Christian world. The obvious question is: What happened between Eusebius' twenty-one book list issued in 325 and Athanasius' list of twenty-seven issued in 367? How did the church finally decide on what to include and what to exclude? Roy Hoover says our sources are mute on this question. However, like other scholars, he suggests that the emperor Constantine's request in 331 for fifty "skillfully executed copies of the divine scripture," finally settled the matter.

The addition of the last six books to the canonical list, Hoover further suggests, was not the result of historical or theological argument but was prompted by the emperor Constantine's desire for a unified state—hence his instruction to Eusebius to produce fifty bibles for churches in Constantinople. While the fourth-century canon has been durable, it has never been universal. Eastern Orthodox churches continued to have different lists of sacred books reflecting the diversity present before Constantine. For example, the second and third letters of Peter and the book of Revelation are absent from the Syriac version of the New Testament, which dates from the fifth century.[18]

Because great differences existed in the text of the Old Latin manuscripts circulating in the latter part of the fourth century, Pope Damascus (304-84), who relegated Constantinople to a rank second to Rome, decided there was need for an authoritative translation of the Bible into Latin. The pope's secretary Jerome (342-420), "the most capable biblical scholar of his day,"[19] was chosen for the job. In 384, Jerome presented the first revised text of the four Gospels—the Vulgate; that is, the Common Bible—which became the standard of the Roman Catholic Church and "has been approved and protected by popes down to this day.[20]

In his *Introduction to the New Testament*, biblical scholar and Catholic priest Raymond Collins tells us that, by the end of the fourth century, the various Christian churches were coming to a point at which each recognized that twenty-seven books constituted the canon of the New Testament; that is, a collection accepted as the authoritative norm and criterion of Christian faith and practice. Of course, the canon that finally emerged was selective as well as collective; it contained only a fraction of the Christian literature that had been produced in the early period. The canon we have today, says Collins, reflects a historical judgement as to what essentially constitutes the church. If one wants real insight into early Christian tradition, one ought to study early Christian literature rather than the twenty-seven books which the "accidents of history served to highlight" during the second, third, and fourth centuries. In effect, "the canon of the New Testament must be considered with the utmost seriousness, yet it can be no more simply equated with the canon of truth in our day than it was at the time of Irenaeus."[21]

Nevertheless, the New Testament canon that was adopted after centuries of debate and discourse has served the church well. By defining the New Testament from the various gospels and sacred writings that proliferated in early Christian communities, the church dealt effectively with challenges to orthodoxy and authority. For centuries afterwards, it turned confidently to the authenticated New Testament as the touchstone of faith to settle disputes.

The eighteenth-century intellectual stirrings known as the Enlightenment challenged that confidence. The discrepancies within the Gospels raised the question of which was the oldest and most accurate account of the events surrounding Jesus' life. Just what sources had the Gospel writers used? Until this time, the Bible, church teachings, and church traditions were all considered when defining authority. The radical notion that the Bible alone was the ultimate authority in matters of Christian doctrine, the desire to translate scripture into the language of the common people and to place it into the hands of, in the words of William Tyndale (ca. 1495-1536), the "boye that dryveth the plough," all contributed to a religious upheaval.

Scripture had been translated into English even before the Wycliffe Bible made its dramatic appearance in the last decades of the fourteenth century, "like a mountain among foothills."[22] The eighth-century monk Bede is said to have translated the Gospel of John into Anglo-Saxon. But the first complete translation of the Bible from Latin into English is credited to John Wycliffe (ca. 1330-1384), an English philosopher and Oxford scholar. Wycliffe's work was part of his larger task of reforming the church, earning him the title "Morning Star of the Reformation." Wycliffe argued that just as Jesus and his Apostles taught in the language of the people, the scriptures should be made available to people in a language they fully understood.

Wycliffe and his associates in fact produced two versions of the Bible in English. The first, which appeared about 1380, was condemned as heretical, but the second, which appeared in manuscript form about 1388, after Wycliffe's death, was accepted as "catholic." It was even "recommended for reading by people as indisputably orthodox as Sir Thomas More." But English church authorities did all they could to suppress this English Bible, and its widespread dissemination was curtailed by a decree issued by a synod in Oxford in 1408. This decree forbade the translation or even the reading of the Bible in English without permission.[23] In 1428, to show how they felt about Wycliffe and his Bible, the authorities dug up his body and burned it.

In his 1976 book *The Bible in Early English Literature*, David Fowler says that the controversy surrounding the Wycliffe Bible continues. On one hand, he says, there are those who see Wycliffe as a prophet of the Reformation, whose actual influence, indeed, was one of the forces that produced it. Others are inclined to defend the church, saying that heresy was being condemned and not the translation of the Bible as such.[24]

It was Martin Luther (1483-1546) who did most to wrestle the Bible out of the hands of the clergy and the educated classes and to put it, if not into the hands of the common man, at least within his reach. After the former Augustinian monk launched what was to become known as the Protestant Reformation, he set about translating the Bible into German for a reformed church, much to the disgust of his antagonists. "This is not the Bible," they said. "It is a piece of outright heresy which seeks to blaspheme against God and the Pope. Luther has warped the original to suit his own doctrine."[25] But there was no stopping Luther. He forged ahead with the aid of a new invention called the printing press which, with its movable metal type, had revolutionized the dissemination of written material. Developed by a goldsmith named Johann Gutenburg, the new press had produced the first printed Latin Bible somewhere about 1450. The books of Holy Scripture could now be heard in the vernacular, although it was only with the advent of machines for paper-making and mechanical printing machines in the early nineteenth century that they could be inexpensively produced and widely distributed.[26]

The first "reformer" to translate the Bible into English from the original Greek was not as lucky as Wycliffe. William Tyndale (ca. 1495-1536) the "father of the English Bible," a university scholar from Gloucestershire, England, and an early convert to Lutheranism, paid with his life for his efforts. He was unable to find authorization in England for his translation, and went to Germany in 1524 with financial aid from a London cloth merchant. It must be remembered that while King Henry VIII was to replace the pope as the head of the Reformed Church in England, he had, in 1521, been awarded the title *Fidei Defensor* (Defender of the Faith) by Pope Leo X for his hard-hitting treatise refuting Luther's teachings on the sacraments.

After Cologne's city fathers forbade the printing in their city, Tyndale's translation of the New Testament was printed in Worms in 1526. Copies soon appeared in England and were bought in large numbers by the Bishop of London for public burning. The Lord High Chancellor, Sir Thomas More, who was to be executed later on Henry VIII's orders for refusing to accept the king's supremacy over the Church of England, described the translation as "not worthy to be called Christ's testament, but either Tyndale's own testament or the testament of his master Antichrist."[27] After Tyndale moved to Antwerp, he began work on translating the Old Testament. Betrayed to agents of emperor Charles V, he was arrested, and taken to Vilvorde north of Brussels, and imprisoned. He was tried, found guilty of heresy, and, in October of 1536, executed. Tyndale's efforts to produce a Bible in the language of the people were not in vain. In a preface to the Authorized King James Version of the Bible first published in England in 1611, the translators acknowledged their indebtedness to the earlier work of Tyndale and others by writing that it was not their purpose to "make a new translation ... but to make a good one better."

There were two competing bibles when James VI of Scotland ascended the English throne as James I of England in 1603; the immensely popular 1560 Geneva Bible, translated in the Swiss city for the Protestants who had fled the England of the Catholic monarch Mary; and the 1568 Bishops' Bible, so named for the number of Anglican bishops on the committee. At a 1604 Hampton Court conference of theologians and churchmen, the chief representative of the Puritan cause called for a new translation of the Bible, and James I ordered the work. Seven years later, what was to become known as the Authorized King James Version of the Bible was published. It took decades for it to replace the Geneva Bible in affection of the people, but once it did, it became the Bible of the English-speaking people.

Meanwhile, Roman Catholics who had fled England during the reign of the Protestant Elizabeth I started working on an English New Testament at Rheims in France. Work on the Old Testament was completed at Douay in 1609, and until well into the twentieth century, the Rheims-Douay Bible remained the basis for most of Catholic editions of the Bible in English.

The Roman Catholic Church did not issue an authoritative statement about the contents of the Bible until April 8, 1546, when the Council of Trent, by a split vote of twenty-four to fifteen with sixteen abstentions, declared the writings in Jerome's Latin Vulgate version to be the Church's official canon. The Roman Catholic canon differs, however, from the Bible accepted by most Protestant churches: it includes what is known as the Apocrypha—books disputed by early church fathers—which were omitted in the Old Testament of Protestant Bibles.[28]

That council's action came as a response to Luther's decision to relegate the Epistle to the Hebrews, James, Jude, and Revelation to a lesser stature than that enjoyed by the other twenty-three books, putting them only as an appendix to his German-language New Testament. Underscoring the listing of the twenty-seven books of the New Testament and the forty-five books of the Old Testament, the Council of Trent issued a solemn warning: "If anyone does not accept all these books in their entirety, with all their parts, as they are being read in the Catholic Church and are contained in the ancient Latin Vulgate edition, as sacred and canonical and knowingly and deliberately rejects the aforesaid traditions, anathema sit [let him be accursed]."[29]

One of the questions that has intrigued scholars and theologians down the ages is which of the Synoptic Gospels came first. The Gospels of Matthew, Mark, and Luke are so called because they present a "common view" of Jesus. This distinguishes them from John's Gospel, which was written last and in a totally different style. Which Synoptic Gospel came first has profound implications for our image of Jesus. The fourth-century theologian Augustine said the Gospels originated in the sequence in which they stand in the canon. Matthew was the earliest; Mark was an abridgement of Matthew; and Luke and John were dependent on the earlier ones. However, most scholars today hold that Mark's Gospel was written first. They argue that Matthew and Luke, when writing their Gospels, used a copy of Mark. And they also used a copy of a hypothetical collection of "Sayings of Jesus," called "Q" (a convenient code letter from the German word *Quelle*, meaning "source"). For instance, the Sermon on the Mount is not found in Mark, but it is in Matthew and Luke, which suggests that it was in "Q." This is known as the "two-source hypothesis," popularized by the mid-eighteenth-century German scholar H. J. Holzmann.

Some scholars would give their right arm for a copy of the illusive "Q." If it did exist, who wrote it? Or at least who gathered the oral sayings? What questions would it answer? What questions would it pose? No "Q" manuscript has ever been found, although some are convinced that there must be a copy buried somewhere. The remarkable biblical discoveries of this century suggest that "Q" might be waiting to be found in a desert cave near the Dead Sea or in the dry sands of Egypt.

The exciting chance discovery of the Dead Sea Scrolls sparked lively scholarly debate about their origins and authorship. Neil Asher Silberman, author of *Hidden Scrolls* and a contributing editor to the magazine *Archaeology*, states that these eight hundred separate documents, found in caves near the Dead Sea in the 1940s and 1950s, are among the most intriguing sources of evidence for a new understanding of early Christianity. Unlike the New Testament, which has undergone "centuries of ecclesiastical editing," this huge cache of Hebrew and Aramaic texts, is the only contemporary manuscript evidence of religious thought from first-century Judea that is available to us. It offers an "unparalleled opportunity for scholars to examine the beliefs of at least one group of Jesus' contemporaries."[30]

Some scholars suggest that the earliest Christians were members of the community that produced the scrolls, and that the community's Teacher of Righteousness was none other than Jesus himself or his brother James the Just. Other theories point to a mysterious breakaway Jewish sect known as the Essenes, whose practices resembled those of the early Christians, as the scrolls' authors. Living in isolation between 140 B.C. to A.D. 70, they awaited the Messiah's arrival and hid their library sometime between A.D. 66 and 70, during the Jewish war with Rome.

While scholars such as Princeton professor James Charlesworth dismiss the idea that the scrolls contain evidence to show that Jesus was an Essene, they do point to major similarities between Jesus and sect members. In *Jesus and the Dead Sea Scrolls*, Charlesworth notes that, by examining Jewish documents like the Dead Sea Scrolls that are contemporaneous with Jesus, we find many terms, phrases, and concepts once considered unique to Jesus. This discovery may disappoint those who wish a Jesus who is unique and in no way similar to his Jewish contemporaries or influenced by their thoughts or writings: "Christian theologians for over nineteen hundred years have warned that this line of reasoning is dangerous and denies the truth encapsulated in John 1:14, 'And the Word became flesh and dwelt among us....'"[31]

The assumption that the twenty-seven writings we identify as the New Testament are, as a whole, the earliest Christian writings is one that flies in the face of contemporary scholarship, says New Testament scholar Raymond Collins.[32] Elaine Pagels also points out that the canonical Gospels were not by any means the only accounts of Jesus' life and teaching. While the Apostle Paul appears not to have any interest in collecting Jesus' sayings, other Christians did and began to write them down. Pagels quotes from the Secret Book of James, found among the Nag Hammadi texts discovered in Upper Egypt in 1945: "The twelve disciples were all sitting together at one time and remembering what the saviour said to each one of them, whether secretly or openly, and putting it into books." Most scholars, according to Pagels, agree that a collection of Jesus' sayings, translated from the Aramaic he spoke into Greek, circulated widely during the first century, although we do not have an actual copy of that source.[33]

The accidental 1945 discovery of the fifty-two sacred texts—Coptic translations of Greek originals—that comprise the Nag Hammadi Library was a momentous event in the annals of Christian history. Named after the Egyptian village near where it was found, the Library is a collection of texts from the early centuries of the Christian era, including a collection of previously unknown early Christian gospels. Written by the persecuted "heretical" Gnostics, who denied the full humanity of Jesus Christ, the collection includes sayings that criticize common Christian beliefs, such as the virgin birth or the bodily resurrection, as naive misunderstandings.

Gnosticism was a complex religious movement originating in pagan circles and found in many different forms in the ancient world. Christianity was not immune from this intellectual movement. By the end of the second century, Christian Gnostic sects began to appear. Different teachers, such as Marcion and Valentinus, developed their own form of Gnosticism, but some features were common to all forms. Of primary importance was "gnosis"; that is, the revealed knowledge of God and of the origin and destiny of humankind by means of which the spiritual element in the human person could be redeemed.

Gnosticism distinguished between the supreme, remote, and unknowable Divine Being and the "creator god." The "creator god," originating from the Divine Being, was imperfect and created an imperfect world opposed to the spiritual. The function of Christ was to come as the emissary of the supreme God, bringing secret knowledge that would free the spiritual element. However, Gnostics believed that Christ, as a Divine Being, never assumed a properly human form nor did he die. According to Gnosticism, he either inhabited a human being, Jesus, or assumed a phantasmal human appearance.

Despite aggressive efforts to stamp out the movement, it never abandoned the realm of Christianity, as Pope John Paul II notes. Instead, "it has always existed side by side with Christianity, sometimes taking the shape of a philosophical movement, but more often assuming the characteristics of a religion, or para-religion in distinct, if not declared conflict with all that is essentially Christian."[34]

Elaine Pagels argues that the suppression of the Nag Hammadi texts as banned documents and their burial were part of a struggle critical for the formation of early Christianity. These texts, and others like them that circulated at the beginning of the Christian era, were denounced as heresy by orthodox Christians in the middle of the second century. "We have long known," Pagels says, "that many early followers of Christ were condemned by other Christians as heretics, but nearly all we know about them came from what their opponents wrote attacking them."

Pagels concludes *The Gnostic Gospels* by suggesting that had the Nag Hammadi texts been discovered a thousand years earlier, they would have been burned for heresy. Today, she says, "we read them with different eyes, not merely as 'madness and blasphemy' but as Christians in the first centuries experienced them—a powerful alternative to what we know as orthodox Christian tradition. Only now are we beginning to consider the questions with which they confront us."[35]

Among the Nag Hammadi texts is the Gospel of Thomas, which, for the most part, is a collection of Jesus' sayings with almost no biographical material. Because it enables scholars to cross-check material in the Synoptic Gospels, it is considered crucial for the examination of Christianity's early years and its development. Although challenged by other scholars, Helmut Koester at Harvard suggests that parts of Thomas may predate the Synoptic Gospels.[36]

The Gospel of Thomas is included in the fifteen gospels that make up Robert Miller's *The Complete Gospels*. As well as the four authorized Gospels of Matthew. Mark, Luke, and John, Miller's collection also includes "Q," the Secret Book of James, the Secret Gospel of Mark, and the Gospel of Mary. Miller points out that before Matthew, Mark, Luke, and John were designated as the only orthodox Gospels, many Christians had cherished other gospels, which they sincerely believed to carry the revealed truth about Jesus. It is only from the perspective of later centuries, he writes, that these texts that nourished the faith of generations of Christians can be called non-canonical.[37]

Although excluded from the New Testament, these texts contain and disclose valuable historical information. In some instances, they depict a Jesus and an early Christian community that is far removed from traditional interpretations. For instance, the Gospel of Mary records rivalry between the male disciples and Mary Magdelene, who plays a major role in Gnostic literature. The gospel relates that Peter was furious after learning that the risen Lord had spoken secretly to Mary, suggesting that the Lord surely did not wish to indicate that she was more worthy than the apostles.[38] The same gospel tells us that "the companion of the [Savior is] Mary Magdalene. [But Christ loved] her more than [all] the disciples and used to kiss her [often] on her [mouth]. The rest of [the disciples were offended by it...]. They said to him, 'why do you love her more than all of us?' The Saviour answered and said to them, 'Why do I not love you as [I love] her?'"[39]

The Infancy Gospel of Thomas, not to be confused with the Gospel of Thomas, portrays the young Jesus as a petulant boy who initially uses his powers in a self-serving way. When jostled by another child, Jesus tells him he will not finish his journey. At once, the gospel records, the child fell down and died.[40] Another narrative in this gospel plays on the Jewish unwillingness to accept Jesus as the divine Alpha and Omega. A Jewish teacher, observing Jesus' cleverness, asks his parents to hand him over to him so he can teach Jesus the alphabet. The teacher recites carefully for Jesus all the letters of alphabet from alpha to omega. Jesus responds to the Jewish teacher, "You don't really know the alpha [Christ]; how are you to teach others the beta? You phony, if you knew it, teach the alpha first, and then we'll trust you about the beta."[41]

Miller points out that, until fairly recently, many people interested in Jesus were not even aware of the existence of these and other "extracanonical" gospels, or if they knew about them, did not know where to find them. In recent years, the once-hard-to-find material has been put on the shelves of bookstores, making it readily available to the layperson. While scholars have had access to these documents and could study them in the original languages, Miller says the vast majority of academics tended to dismiss them as unimportant, "on the hasty assumption that all of them were fanciful elaborations" based on the New Testament Gospels or that they came from a much later period.[42]

The true value of these documents continues to be a moot point. "None of these books was ever taken seriously by the early Church, and the really bad ones were condemned officially by bishops," says Kevin Orlin Johnson in his 1994 book *Why Do Catholics Do That?* "Even today, a few of these bizarre books survive, and some academic-sounding authors still try to use them to expose Christianity as a garble of everybody else's old myths. Somehow they always fail to mention that the Church has insisted from the first that these spurious texts have nothing to do with Christianity."[43]

Research in the last several decades has significantly broadened understanding of the diversity, and the complexity, of the early Jesus traditions. Scholars now find it necessary to turn to the extracanonical gospels to learn about the development of even the earliest Jesus traditions. For researchers and teachers everywhere, these gospels, which contain traditions independent of the New Testament Gospels, represent significant pieces in the Jesus mosaic. Like the period of the Enlightenment, these new discoveries have convinced many Christians that there is more to the story than what is in the Bible: that a distinction can be made between the texts of scripture and the history behind it.

To this day, says Yale University Divinity School professor David Bartlett, Christians adjudicate that difference in varied ways. Some Christians want to maintain that "the distinction itself is a confusion infecting the church from alien humanism." They contend that the Gospels are history and, read in the right way, state historical facts about Jesus. These Christians are apt to claim that reading the Gospels as biography presents no problems, though "of course the complicated harmonizations and interpretations to which they often resort show they are mired in a very great problem indeed."

At the other extreme, Bartlett notes that other Christians influenced by, but moving beyond, Rudolf Bultmann (one of this century's most prominent New Testament scholars) have held that the stories about Jesus and the early preaching do tell us who God is and how we can relate to God in faith. In this judgement, however, "faith is not dependent on any historical research, not even the research that assures us that there was a Jesus of Nazareth." Most of those Christians, Bartlett says, do not deny that Jesus was a historical figure, but they do not believe that his historicity is a requirement of faith.[44]

Dissenting Voices 5

T he quest for the historical Jesus—that figure of history stripped of layers of interpretation—can be a daunting task, even for scholars equipped with all the tools of historical research. For the layperson, it can be a bewildering, frustrating project full of twists and turns, detours, and roadblocks. Where to start? What to read? Who to believe?

Fortunately, scholars have divided the quest into three periods: the Old Quest, from the early eighteenth century to the early decades of the twentieth century; the New Quest, from the mid-twentieth century to the 1970s; and the Third Quest, starting about 1980 and continuing today. The first two quests were dominated by German Protestant scholars, while the Third Quest is primarily a North America phenomenon and includes both Protestant and Roman Catholic scholars.

To understand what motivated scholars to search for the historical Jesus, it is necessary to understand the current of events that tugged at their imaginations, prompting them to re-examine and challenge the validity of long-held ideas and beliefs.

By the twelfth century, the Christian church appeared unshakeable and invincible, but, as historian Kenneth Clarke notes, "round it was a play of minds, a tugging and a tension that has hardly existed since." It was an age of intense intellectual activity. For instance, in about 1130, Peter Abelard, whose rationalism in theology had been condemned by the church, risked excommunication when he proclaimed: "I must understand in order to believe. By doubting we come to question, and by questioning we perceive the truth."[1]

Nicolaus Copernicus (1473-1543) and Galileo Galilei (1564-1613) questioned, perceived the truth, and shook the very heavens when they proved that the earth was not the centre of the universe. Their startling heliocentric theory that put the sun and not the earth at the centre was condemned by the church, not, suggests theologian Karen Armstrong, because it endangered belief in God the Creator, but because it contradicted the word of God in scripture. Their theory certainly raised some interesting questions. How could the theory that the earth moved around the sun be reconciled with such biblical verses as "The world also is established, that it cannot be moved"? If, as Galileo suggested, there could be human life on the moon, how could these men have descended from Adam and how had they got out of Noah's Ark?[2] What did it mean for the concept of original sin and the redemptive power of Jesus' suffering and death?

By challenging belief solidly anchored in scripture, men of science sowed the seeds of doubt that were to mature into outright assaults on the Christian faith, the Bible's authenticity, and the very nature of Jesus Christ himself. If the stars and tides moved without divine intervention, could thinking people hope for such intervention in their own affairs? What if theological theories turned out to be as faulty as theories about universe?[3] The advent of book-printing during the Renaissance and the "humanists' longing to go back to the sources and search for truth" in the time of the Reformation and Counter-Reformation added to a radical new way of looking at and examining the Bible.[4]

The Renaissance, that flowering of art, literature, and learning that began in Italy in the fourteenth century, contributed to a bold, fresh, new vision of life. It marked the transition from the medieval world to the modern. This movement focused attention on individual expression, self-consciousness, and worldly experiment. Fine libraries and universities flourished, and scholars, poets, and artists were supported by such great patrons as the Medici family of Florence. Although sometimes perceived as an anti-religious movement, the Renaissance was rooted in Christian thought. As historian Kenneth Clarke notes, a few humanists had shown signs of scepticism but none had expressed any doubts about the Christian religion as a whole.[5]

However, by the sixteenth century, the voice of dissent began to be heard ever more loudly. It was not raised against religion as such, but against what was perceived as an abuse of authority by the church of Rome which was, we must remember, the one authority for Western Christianity. To the East, the Orthodox hierarchy ordered faith and practice. One such dissenting voice was that of the Dutchman Desiderius Erasmus (1466/69-1536), scholar and Christian humanist. A decade after the turn of the century, as Pope Julius II laid the foundation stone of the new St. Peter's in Rome, Erasmus attacked corruption in the church.

But it was the Augustinian monk Martin Luther, that "wild boar loose in the Lord's vineyards," who really turned things upside down. In 1517, outraged by the sale of indulgences by the Dominican friar Johann Tetzel, Luther challenged Rome with a list of ninety-five criticisms of church practices and so launched what came to be known as the Protestant Reformation. By translating the Bible into German, Luther gave the people "not only a chance to read Holy Writ themselves, but the tools of thought."[6] He threw down the gauntlet and changed the face of hierarchical Christianity, until then centred in Rome. However, as scholars point out, Luther's complaints were directed at what he believed to be the unnecessary overlays in Christian belief and practice that had accumulated during the Middle Ages; he was not testing the authenticity of the claims put forward by Christian scriptures.

Luther, who was excommunicated in 1521, remained true to the orthodoxy proclaimed by such church councils as Nicaea and Chalcedon. Indeed, according to Karen Armstrong, his theory of justification depended upon the divinity of Christ and his Trinitarian status: "These traditional doctrines of God were too deeply embedded in the Christian experience for either Luther or Calvin to question."[7]

Luther may have remained true to church orthodoxy but the Reformation he helped start unsettled men's minds and shattered Christian unity. As the printing presses turned out a proliferation of books and pamphlets, religion became as much a matter for discussion and debate in the marketplace as the crops and the weather. The voice of the cleric was no longer accepted as the voice of authority. As a result, the Reformation split Christianity into a plethora of squabbling sects and sparked bloody wars, pitting Catholic against Protestant and Protestant against Protestant. Dogma, rather than decreasing, actually increased as alternative interpretations of Christianity claimed authenticity. Rival groups condemned each other as well as unbelief.

Luther's doctrine of justification by faith alone instead of by sacrament, good works, and mediation placed man in direct communication with God. He insisted that the reading of the Bible placed a greater responsibility on the individual for his or her own salvation. This emphasis on the individual rather than on the church hierarchy was to be embraced later by a movement which espoused a rational, moderate Christianity. The movement was called Deism.

It was the Deists—rationalists with a hunger for religion—and the Enlightenment thinkers who called into question some of Christianity's central tenets. Attacking traditional sources of Christianity, such as the Bible and the church, as highly unreliable, they planted doubt in the minds of an increasingly literate population, clearing the way for challenges to the orthodox view of Jesus.

The Deist movement, which found expression in England and Europe and later in North America, is said to have taken its lead from the Englishman Charles Blount. Blount was the journalist son of a Herdfordshire knight who died in 1693, a year before the birth of Herman Samuel Reimarus, who was to become a shining beacon of historical Jesus research. A thorn in the side of the clergy, Blount pestered them with such questions as, "How was it light before the sun was made?" and "Where did Eve get the thread with which she sewed her fig leaves together?"[8]

Accepting the Bible as allegorical, Deists tended to reject faith, mystery, revelation, and the divine inspiration of scripture. Pointing to inconsistencies in the Gospels and in early church accounts, Deists argued the case against prophecy and miracles and rejected such things as the resurrection. Instead, they appealed to a natural religion, rationally deducible from the evidence of the natural world and man's unchanging conscience. The 1730 publication *Christianity as Old as Creation,* by the Englishman Matthew Tindal, is often known as the Deist Bible, calling as it did for a new understanding of Jesus. Tindal argued that, in the light of new understanding, the so-called miracle recorded in the Gospels could no longer prove the uniqueness of Jesus and the validity of his message.

By the eighteenth century, challenges to Christian dogma are said to have intensified to such a degree that, in 1736, Joseph Butler, the Anglican Bishop of Durham, lamented that "it is come, I know not how, to be taken for granted by many persons, that Christianity is now at length discovered to be fictitious."[9] So rapid was the spread of Deist opinions that by 1760 many of the leading men in the Church of England, particularly among the London clergy, were said to be Deist in their private belief.

The Enlightenment, or the Age of Reason, with its spirit of scepticism, rationalism, empiricism, and outright disbelief, hammered a further nail in orthodoxy's coffin. According to Steve Mason, it sparked a massive effort to recover the human qualities of the church's sacred writings. Gospel criticism, he says, was "in part a product of the emerging discipline of history: in part it was the anvil on which the discipline was hammered out."[10]

Enlightenment thinkers argued that the truth of religion is determined from reason not from revelation, and eighteenth-century scholars started asking about the source of the Gospels. Just where did the Gospel writers get their information? Aided by the secular sciences, especially history, archaeology, and philology, scholars struggled to provide an answer. And, as Jaroslav Pelikan notes, the quest of the historical Jesus was not confined to biblical and theological scholars. In the later part of the eighteenth century and the early part of the nineteenth, the quest became at least as much a vocation of other intellectual disciplines.

In a search for new ways to "understand reality, to validate morality, and to organize society now that the old orthodoxy had been discredited," these scholars undertook to reinterpret the major classics of Western culture in a manner that would make their "abiding message available to an new age." The Enlightenment scholars who searched for the historical Jesus, Pelikan says, were engaged in what might be called the quest for the historical Homer and the quest for the historical Socrates as well as the quest for the historical Moses.[11] It meant that under the microscope of biblical criticism, Jesus and scripture were subject to the same scrutiny as any other set of documents and historical figures.

The Jesus of Nazareth who actually lived in first-century Palestine, unrestricted by the doctrinal presentations of him in Bible, creed, and church, was the goal of these early scholars. As a result, the goal itself established a dichotomy between the orthodox Christ, known through faith and doctrine, and the "real Jesus of Nazareth," who could be discovered through the scientific method.[12]

In any chronicle of the search for the historical Jesus, the name Herman Samuel Reimarus (1694-1768) is writ large. Although he had predecessors, the Hamburg-born scholar who became a professor of Hebrew and oriental languages, is credited with initiating the first of the three quests that, each in their own way, questioned long-held theological assumptions. A child of the Enlightenment, Reimarus was born into a family of Lutheran clergy in the waning years of the tumultuous seventeenth century—a century marked by new attitudes toward all established authorities and by a storm of dissenting voices that shook the tree of faith to its roots. He is said to have been tormented from his youth by the "irreconcilable contradiction between the conclusions of reason and the demand of faith." If God wanted to teach mankind by dictating the Holy Scriptures, why had he made them so obscure? If all who were damned were damned forever, why did Christians think of their God as a God of love and of Jesus as a bringer of salvation? These were some of the questions with which he grappled. Finally, driven by a fierce honesty, Reimarus abandoned Christianity. He did so reluctantly, compelled by reason.[13]

By challenging the authority of scripture, Reimarus distinguished between what Jesus taught and what the Gospels said about him suggesting that "Christianity was a fabrication created out of the conniving minds of Jesus' followers."[14] His perspective revolutionized the image of Jesus in modern theology and became a point of departure for Albert Schweitzer's pivotal *The Quest of the Historical Jesus*, published in 1906. In paying homage to Reimarus' contribution to the search for the historical Jesus, Schweitzer noted that "before Reimarus, no one had attempted to form a historical conception of the life of Jesus." He also noted that the only life of Jesus of interest to him that was penned prior to Reimarus was written in the Persian language by a Jesuit missionary in India. Schweitzer dismissed this "life" as a skilful falsification.[15]

Reimarus, who was influenced by Deists he had met in England and in Holland,[16] put his thoughts down in manuscript form, which is believed to have been written for private circulation. Given that the work rejected miracles and revelation, and "sought to convict the biblical writers of conscious fraud, innumerable contradictions, and fanaticism," it is perhaps understandable that fragments of his work were not published until ten years after his death and then only anonymously.[17] Taken by themselves, the fragments were radical yet familiar to anyone versed in Deist thought. However, when placed together they amounted to a scandal. It was the fragment "Concerning the Goal of Jesus and his Disciples" that had the most devastating and lasting effect. It portrayed Jesus as a failed Messianic pretender, whose disciples, after his death, revised the story of his life to fit their own purposes. In other words, the Gospels are falsifications and historical Christianity is a gigantic deception.

The fragments were published by another name highlighted in the quest of the historical Jesus: Gotthold Lessing (1729-81), a former dramatist and theatre manager who at one time was librarian to the Duke of Brunswick. Lessing, who thrived on controversy and cherished debate as the blood line of culture, was plunged into the most sustained and most acrimonious dispute of his life. Reimarus' work and Lessing's own theoretical writings on the subject laid the foundations of Protestant liberalism that was to hold sway through the nineteenth century.[18]

Fifty-four years after Lessing's death, the theological world was shaken by the publication of the massive *The Life of Christ Critically Examined* by the German university professor David Friedrich Strauss (1808-74). This publication, "the theological book of the century ... the book that made him famous and destroyed his career,"[19] created a furore by explaining away the divinity of Christ. Advocating what he called a mythological approach, Strauss called for an appreciation of the Gospel miracle stories as narratives "composed by early Christians to express their faith in Jesus as the Messiah sent in fulfillment of the promises made to Israel."[20] Strauss also argued that it was impossible to write a life of Jesus, both "because the Gospels refused to see Jesus simply as a part of history and because the Gospels give us only unconnected fragments, the order being imposed by the Evangelists."[21]

Because of Strauss' book, the year 1835 has been called the "great revolutionary year of modern theology," and Strauss himself, in the words of Swiss theologian Karl Barth (1886-1968), became "infamously famous." The dubious fame cost Strauss his career and forced him to abandon his teaching post at the prestigious Tübingen University. Based on his own research, Strauss, at the end of his life, had to say "no" to the question "Are we still Christians?" For him, says German Professor of New Testament, Gerd Lüdemann, "the elements of the Christ myth had dissolved and not much more could be said of Jesus than his enthusiasm."[22]

The second half of the nineteenth century saw the production, particularly in Germany, of a steady stream of books on the search for the historical Jesus. One of the most influential was *The Synoptic Gospels: Their Origin and Historical Character* by H. J. Holzmann (1832-1910), a professor of New Testament in Heidelberg. Holzmann postulated the "Two Source" Theory—that Mark's Gospel and the hypothetical sayings source known as "Q" were used by the evangelists Matthew and Luke. This "two source" theory today remains the basis for most scholars in their critical examination of the Gospels of Matthew, Mark, and Luke.

Theologian N. Thomas Wright suggests that by giving priority to Mark, Holzmann developed a hypothesis "designed to provide a straightforward (and essentially liberal) portrait of Jesus as the teacher of timeless ethical truths,"[23] whose ministry developed in clear-cut and comprehensible stages with the decisive turning point at Caesarea Philippi when he asked his disciples "Who do people say that I am?" Peter answered, "You are the Messiah," and Jesus sternly ordered his disciples not to tell anyone about him (Mark 8:27-30). Up to this point, the Gospel tells us, Jesus called his disciples, spoke with authority, and performed miracles. After this point, Jesus tells his disciples that the son of Man must suffer and die, and on the third day, rise again.

Meanwhile, four years before Holzmann's monumental work, the English naturalist Charles Darwin (1809-1882) published his *Origin of Species* (1859), which suggested that higher forms of life had descended from lower forms. The book was so popular that its first edition sold out in one day and it precipitated raging controversies in the world of science and religion. Darwin challenged the natural order as proclaimed by scripture by exposing the biblical account of creation as incompatible with natural selection. Darwin's book was to have a profound influence on concepts of life, the universe, and Christianity. Twelve years later, for much the same reasons, his *The Descent of Man* cast further doubts on the veracity of the Scriptures as historical documents.

Questions about how far the Scriptures could be used as historical tools were also raised by the archaeological advances of the nineteenth century, with their emphasis on disengaging fact from fiction. As Dead Sea Scrolls scholar Neil Asher Silberman notes, until the last century, the most common images of the seas and rolling hills of Galilee had far more to do with faith than with topographical reality. Gradually, however, a first-hand knowledge of Galilean geography became an essential part of New Testament history and scholarship.[24]

An important first step was taken by the Frenchman Ernest Renan (1823-92), who had entered a seminary intending to become a Roman Catholic priest and later renounced his vocation after having been influenced by German biblical scholarship to question the literal truth of Christian teaching. In 1860, he accompanied Napoleon III's invasion force into Lebanon and carried out brief excavations along the Phoenician coast. After travelling through the villages of southern Lebanon and Galilee, Renan published his own *Life of Jesus* in 1863, the first work in a series called *History of the Origins of Christianity*. Renan's *Life of Jesus*, which cause a sensation after it was published, stripped Christianity of its supernatural trappings and presented Jesus as a man, albeit an incomparable man. Because of the controversy stirred up by his best-selling book, Renan was removed from his professorship at the College de France.

The fallout from Renan's book, considered scandalous by most Christians of the time, was far-reaching and is said to have contributed to the Roman Catholic Church's anti-Modernist purge. In 1893, a year after Renan's death, the French biblical scholar Alfred Loisy (1857-1940) fell victim to the purge when he was dismissed from his teaching post at the Parisian Institut Catholique because of his unorthodox views and was later excommunicated, in 1908. Like other scholars, Loisy advocated a critical look at the Bible: that it be interpreted as any other historical document rather than as an uncritically accepted expression of faith. In his most important work, *The Gospel and the Church*, written in 1902, Loisy denied that the church was founded by Christ in the form it later assumed. In later works he "disassociated the historical Jesus, unconscious of his divinity, and the Christ of faith, and sees the early Christian community as a screen between believer and event."[25]

In a further crackdown on "unorthodox" views, Pope Pius X (1903-14) issued an encyclical, or pastoral, letter, denouncing Modernism as heresy and opposing all scholarship that questioned the early history of Christianity. By 1910, an anti-Modernist oath had been imposed upon the clergy everywhere but in Germany. With a few exceptions, the Modernist scare effectively put the haul to biblical scholarship and Jesus research in Roman Catholic circles until the pontificate of Pius XII.

In German Protestant circles of the late eighteenth century, however, the quest of the historical Jesus was not dampened. Many scholars believed that Holzmann's "two source" theory would solve the problem of the historical Jesus. But it was not to be. In 1901, William Wrede's (1859-1906) book *The Messianic Secret* argued that the dilemma of historical Jesus research lay in the very nature of the sources themselves.[26] In his "scandalous" book, the German professor of the New Testament took issue with the liberal theologians of his day who believed that the proof of Jesus' Messiahship was contained in Mark's Gospel, which they considered the earliest narrative. He argued that Jesus' Messiahship was the creation of a post-resurrection Christian community and was then incorporated by Mark into his Gospel. In other words, Mark was writing not as an objective historian but from the viewpoint of Christian faith. Wrede's book jolted the liberals' optimistic quest for the Jesus of history.

A few years later, Albert Schweitzer (1875-1965) was to administer an even more damaging blow. The eldest son of an ordained Lutheran pastor, Schweitzer was a man of relentless energy and many talents—as philosopher, theologian, musician. He is perhaps best known for his medical missionary work in French Equatorial Africa, out of which grew his reverence-for-all-life philosophy. He was awarded the Nobel Peace Prize in 1952 for his humanitarian work.

Schweitzer's contribution to historical Jesus research was enormous. His first book, *The Mystery of the Kingdom of God* (1901), propounded what was to become the essential theme of his theological work: that Christ's life and teaching could only be interpreted in the light of his and his contemporaries' belief in the imminent end of the world.[27] This theme was further developed in his 1906 publication of *The Quest of the Historical Jesus*, which tied together more than a century of disparate life of Jesus research and became a landmark for the development of much Protestant thinking. After reviewing the major works on the historical Jesus from Reimarus to Wrede, Schweitzer concluded that further attempts to write books on the life of the historical Jesus would be futile.

Although a devout Christian who believed in Jesus' divinity, Schweitzer argued that modern biographies of Jesus aimed "at influencing the Christian community by giving a complete impression of the life of Jesus, a life which even for the disciples according to the gospel writers remained a mystery."[28] According to him, the half-historical and half-modern depictions of Jesus by eighteenth-century authors only "served theology by painting a portrait which they could use to their ends." Future biographies of Jesus would paint a entirely different portrait than in the past. This future Jesus would not be the cherished Jesus of established religion, nor would he be a figure created by "popular historical treatment," sympathetic and universally intelligible to the masses. "The historical Jesus will be to our time a stranger and an enigma."[29]

What was Schweitzer really saying? In his 1956 book *Jesus of Nazareth*, Günther Bornkamm, professor of New Testament at the University of Heidelberg, suggests that Schweitzer had concluded that no one could write a life of Jesus in the old style. This conclusion, said Bornkamm, spelled the end of almost two hundred years of prodigious effort to regain and expound the life of the historical Jesus, freed from all embellishment by dogma and doctrine. In Bornkamm's words, "Schweitzer had erected a memorial to the work that had gone before while at the same time delivering its funeral oration."[30]

Summing up the Old Quest, theologian N. Thomas Wright says that, in their different ways, Reimarus, Strauss, and Schweitzer undertook historical description to show that the traditional picture of Jesus could not be trusted: Reimarus went on to argue that Christianity as a whole was mistaken; Strauss argued that its reality lay in the "realm of timeless truth divorced from history"; and, according to Schweitzer, "the new historical picture carried with it its own timeless imperatives." For Wright, the subsequent story of the quest of the historical Jesus is not least the story of how scholars variously met the challenge of making "such a strange and remote Jesus relevant in a different culture and time."[31]

"The More, the Merrier" | 6

In an August 1994 review of three current "Jesus" books, Leander E. Keck of Yale Divinity School introduced his article with the words, "The historical Jesus is back. For the third time, we are told." How did this come about? Keck argues that the first quest of the historical Jesus foundered when it became apparent that the Gospels of Matthew, Mark, Luke, and their sources were so thoroughly permeated by theological intent and interpretation of the evangelists that Jesus the man could be glimpsed only here and there. Furthermore, the historical Jesus that *could* be recovered turned out to be an apocalyptic preacher of the kingdom of God—a figure "as alien to liberal Protestantism as to the Christ of dogma."[1]

Schweitzer's requiem for the nineteenth-century quest was to have a inescapable impact on the mood of historical Jesus research in the twentieth century. In fact, it could be said that Schweitzer's work helped introduce a "no quest" period of almost fifty years. Schweitzer anticipated this "no quest" period by saying that the historical Jesus he had discovered was, for the most part, insignificant for twentieth century faith and practice.[2] Schweitzer's own words sum up his position: "... the truth is, it is not Jesus as historically known, but Jesus as spiritually arisen within men, who is significant for our time and can help it. Not the historical Jesus, but the spirit which goes forth from Him and in the spirits of men strives for new influence and rule, is that which overcomes the world."[3]

So it appears that shortly after the turn of the century, Schweitzer rendered Jesus as a historical figure insignificant for later generations[4] and the so-called "quest for the historical Jesus" bogged down in negativism. For an influential German school of Protestant theologians, the Gospels were to be taken as theological rather than as historical documents, and they could yield no authentic information about the life and deeds, or even the saying and teachings, of Jesus.[5]

The towering figure in twentieth-century New Testament scholarship who dominated the period of the "no quest" and whose influence still echoes today is German New Testament scholar Rudolf Bultmann (1884-1976). According to Bultmann, the primitive church had little interest in the presentation of a historical life of Jesus when they collected material about him. These collections were motivated, in Bultmann's words, by "propaganda." And, the motivation was primary theological. Therefore, Bultmann concluded that the "Christ who is preached is not the historic Jesus, but the Christ of faith" and Christian worship.[6] This appeared to confirm the impossibility of the quest of the historical Jesus, leading to the inevitable conclusion that the historical Jesus was not essential for the Christian faith. The key element was what Bultmann called an "existential encounter with Christ," which did not depend upon any intellectual critical process but rather a leap into the dark; an acceptance of faith on trust.[7]

James N. Robinson, who was to coin the phrase "new quest," says that the repudiation of the quest for the historical Jesus at the opening of the century found its "definitive crystallization" in Bultmann's scholarship. Despite Bultmann's reputation as a giant of theology, Robinson remembers him as a modest, self-effacing person who never threw his weight around. He wasn't the "wily dangerous kind of person that people often assume when they think about his threatening ideas such as the demythologizing of Jesus."[8]

In his later years, Bultmann was held in warm regard by his former students, many of whom had themselves become professors. One such devotee wished to bring his doctoral students to see the ageing New Testament sage. Bultmann declined and replied wryly, "I am not yet a museum piece." Even his death in 1976 at the age of ninety-two was an occasion for good-natured controversy. Those who revered Bultmann said his longevity was proof of God's blessings upon his theories; those less enamoured of his teaching suggested that his longevity was due to God's uncertainty: God was not sure what to do with Bultmann after he died.

New movements are known and thought by many in various places, then someone gives them voice. In this sense, the end of the "no quest" period is set on a brisk fall day in 1953, when German professor Ernst Käsemann delivered a ground-breaking lecture at Jugendheim, Germany. The second or "new" quest of the historical Jesus was born. In that lecture, before a gathering of Rudolf Bultmann's former students, Käsemann took issue with Bultmann, who argued that the quest for the historical Jesus was not only impossible but illegitimate because the Gospels were composed, if that word may be used, decades after Jesus' death.

Käsemann accepted Schweitzer's conclusion that a "life of Jesus," in the modern sense of a biography, could not be written because so little is known about the historical Jesus. Only the "uncontrolled imagination" could have the self-confidence to weave, out of the pitiful threads of Jesus' life found in the Gospels, "the fabric of a history."[9] However, Käsemann also rejected the historical scepticism generated by Bultmann's conclusions, which had contributed so much to the disinterest in Jesus of Nazareth. Was there not some central point around which something like a life of Jesus could be constructed? Is there a recognizable continuity between early believers' "good news" about Jesus and the message of the historical Jesus himself? This question of continuity became central in the new quest.

Käsemann suggested that there was relatively firm ground to conclude that a Jesus tradition went back to the historical Jesus. In this renewed quest, the criterion of "dissimilarity" became a standard method adopted by scholars to assess the authenticity of Jesus' sayings. Using this criterion, scholars isolate sayings of Jesus considered reasonably authentic from Jewish tradition and early church teachings.[10] An example is Jesus' use of the word "Father" (Aramaic: *Abba*) to address God. It is found in Luke's version of the Lord's Prayer and on Jesus' lips when he prays before his death in the garden of Gethsemane.[11] Many scholars would say that this form of address was not customary among Jews of Jesus' time; they preferred "Our Heavenly Father" or a similar expression. Matthew, and the early church that followed him, reverted to this Jewish form of address. With the influx of Gentile converts, the Aramaic word *Abba* slowly disappeared, found only in fleeting references in Paul's letters to the Romans and the Galatians.[12]

The renewed interest in Jesus sparked by Käsemann's lecture was popularized by Günther Bornkamm's book, *Jesus of Nazareth*. This work disregarded Jesus' miracles, and shunned anything that smacked of a "life" or "biography" of Jesus. Under the influence of Bultmann, Bornkamm regarded the miracles narrated in the Gospels, not as remarkable historical occurrences, but as miracles of Jesus, seen through the eyes of the early church: "Their purpose is hardly biographical in the strict sense. The miraculous deeds are not proofs of [Jesus'] character but of his messianic authority, or his divine power."[13]

Bornkamm showed only the slightest interest in the apparent sequence of historical events narrated by the evangelists. And he showed a mere passing interest in the question as to whether Jesus thought of himself as "Messiah." Behind the doctrine of Jesus' Messiahship, "there still dimly emerges the fact that Jesus' history was originally a non-Messianic history." The Messianic faith of the early Christians was awakened only after Easter by Jesus' words and actions.[14]

Because it helped trigger a new wave of research, and gave momentum to a new quest of the historical Jesus, Bornkamm's book is still popular and remains required reading for theological and divinity students in seminaries throughout the world. In this new quest, the burden of proof rested upon those who insisted that the Gospels were biographies and originated with Jesus in his earthly ministry.[15] It was to produce myriad images of Jesus: prophet, Pharisee, Rabbi, and, inevitably in our time, magician and homosexual.[16]

After Käsemann and Bornkamm, historical Jesus research experienced sporadic bursts of energy during the 1950s, 1960s, and 1970s. Overall, however, it lacked sparkle. As James Robinson notes, Bultmann's scepticism resulted in scholars being more interested in talking about the idea of the historical Jesus than in actually portraying him. As a result, much that was written in this period was "colorless, respectable, responsible, and boring research."[17] The new, or second, quest of the historical Jesus fizzled out with more of a whimper than a bang.

Robinson claims that the "third quest" began in the unlikely location of a Los Angeles hotel balcony. In 1972, during the annual meeting of the Society of Biblical Literature, society members met on the balcony to discuss a seminar on Jesus' parables. Among them were Robert Funk and Dominic Crossan, who would later found the Jesus Seminar. Around this time, scholars were beginning to show renewed interest in the sayings of Jesus contained in "Q," the hypothetical source said to be used by Matthew and Luke. And all this coincided with new archaeological discoveries that suggested Galilee was more Hellenistic than previously thought.

The development and widespread use of new multi-disciplinary methods, a burst of publications, and the establishment of several new professional organizations, such as the Jesus Seminar, saw the third quest of the historical Jesus blossom in the 1980s. It has added up to a new, radical, even revolutionary, image of Jesus. It has shattered the prevailing scholarly consensus that at the centre of Jesus' message and mission was his expectation of the imminent end of the world; it became clear that the "end-of-world" consensus had collapsed. A majority of Jesus scholars—in North American, anyway—no longer thought that Jesus expected the end of the world in his generation.

What has emerged is the conviction that what we can know with the greatest degree of certainty about the pre-Easter Jesus is that he spoke in parables and aphorisms. He was a teller of subversive short stories and a "speaker of provocative one liners that consistently undermine the assumptions of his world and invited his hearers into an alternative perception and way of life."[18]

Perhaps the most striking feature of the third quest, suggests N. Thomas Wright, is its current open-endedness and the publication of a large number of books offering a "bewildering range of competing hypotheses." Although there are some unifying elements, there is no unifying theological agenda, no final agreement about method, and no common set of results.[19] For example, the intriguing question of "Jewishness" is a subject of lively debate.

In the past, scholars interested in the historical Jesus emphasized the "Jewishness" of the Galileans: they were loyal to the temple and Pharisaic in temperament, revolutionary, and awaiting a Messiah who would deliver them from Roman domination and usher in the end of time. However, archaeological evidence unearthed in the late 1970s and early 1980s suggested that the traditional picture of the social and cultural climate in Galilee at the time of Jesus was misleading. Archaeologists Eric M. Meyer and James F. Strange presented a picture of southern Galilee that was open to Hellenistic culture and commerce, predominantly Greek-speaking, and probably bilingual. Only after the Jewish War and the destruction of Jerusalem in A.D. 70 was there a great influx and settlement of Jews in Galilee. All this supported the view that Jesus' world was less Jewish and more Hellenistic than previously supposed.[20]

Recent archaeological investigations suggest that Jesus was influenced by the Hellenistic milieu of cities in Galilee such as Sephoris, which was within walking distance of his hometown, Nazareth. However, N. Thomas Wright argues that Jesus Seminar scholars and others have exaggerated Jesus' contact with Hellenism. "The jury is still out on that one," he says, pointing to Richard Horsley's recent publication on Galilee.

Horsley, New Testament professor at Harvard University, is of the opinion that there were "significant differences" in cultural traditions between official Jerusalem and ordinary people in Galilee, but the situation there was extremely complex. Although Galileans resisted the demands of the priestly establishment in Jerusalem, they had "popular sensitivity" for fundamental Jewish symbols such as circumcision or the Jewish Law. For example, many joined in a peasant strike when the emperor Gaius attempted to place a bust of himself in the Jerusalem Temple.[21]

Wright suspects ideological motives behind the present quest to find a Jesus who was influenced more by Hellenism. His hunch is that Jesus Seminar members and their followers are desperate to find a basically non-Jewish Jesus. Such a Jesus, who criticized the social and religious institutions and proclaimed a new social order that meant an end to mediators and hierarchies, would certainly find a following among today's modern Christians, who are discontent with their own ecclesiastical institutions. Wright sounds the alarm for conservative Christians about this liberal presentation: "The last few times we tried to find a non-Jewish Jesus, it was 'look out all'. This is not good news."[22]

How Jewish was Jesus? That is one of the pivotal questions of the third quest for the historical Jesus. Scholars answer that question in different ways. Geza Vermes, a noted Oxford authority on the Dead Sea Scrolls, sees Jesus as a Jewish charismatic preacher and miracle worker and depicts him, not as a Pharisee, Essene, Zealot or Gnostic, but as a Galilean "holy miracle-worker."[23] Vermes rests his case on the fact that there were other contemporary religious figures, men of God similar to Jesus, who lived in poverty, healed the sick, and cast out devils.

Some scholars are sympathetic to Vermes' picture of Jesus, but not all agree. While Bruce Chilton agrees that Vermes' identification of Jesus as a Hasid or a holy man would be difficult to deny, he points out that because "Hasid" simply means "faithful," it does not mean that Jesus belonged to a group of figures known as the Hassidim. Chilton's own book, *A Galilean Rabbi and His Bible*, expresses his view of Jesus as a wandering teacher who had as his central focus an "understanding of the kingdom of God which he saw as transforming Israel."[24]

E. P. Sanders has taken the quest down a different road, and many claim that his 1985 book *Jesus and Judaism* marks a watershed in historical Jesus research. Rather than seeking to understand Jesus from the few sayings that scholarly consensus considers authentic, Sanders believes that the key to the reconstruction of the historical Jesus lies in his behaviour and activities, particularly the temple controversy. He views Jesus as a prophet in the tradition of Jewish thinking about God's promise of the restoration of Israel. Jesus' action in the temple in Jerusalem, where he cast out the moneylenders, is the cornerstone of Sanders' Jesus. Jesus is one who believes that in the near future God will intervene in history and build a new or renewed temple. He and his disciples will then oversee a Messianic kingdom centred in Jerusalem. "Jesus," says Sanders, "saw himself as God's last messenger before the establishment of the kingdom. He looked for new order, created by a mighty act of God." In this new order, the twelve tribes would be reassembled, there would be a new temple, force of arms would not be needed, divorce would be neither necessary nor permitted, the outcasts, even the wicked, would have a place, and "Jesus and his disciples—the poor, meek and lowly—would have the leading role."[25]

However, for all those scholars who see Jesus primarily as a Jewish prophet, there are others who distance Jesus from his Jewish roots. For instance, New Testament scholar Burton L. Mack argues that, in the light of recent scholarship on Jesus' teaching, "the prevailing opinion about his social role in Galilee needs to be revised." Jesus did not act as a prophet, nor was he an end-of-time figure. Instead, "the social historian recognizes traits that suggest another role. The figure that immediately comes to mind is that of the popular philosopher known as the Cynic."

Cynics belonged to the broadly Socratic tradition and carried on conversations about "life in its social context." Many Cynics espoused a simple life, were well read, and made a profession of criticizing social and religious institutions. Others, however, "lived on the edges of society, made an art of begging, and looked for opportunities to display the virtues of an unencumbered existence at the expense of stuffy convention." Cynics "were a social phenomenon of the times," best known for their cunning "pointed remarks and behavior." Mack points out that "Jesus' use of parables, aphorisms and clever rejoinders is very similar to the Cynics' way with words. Many of his themes are familiar Cynic themes. and his style of social criticism, diffident and vague, also agrees with the typical Cynic stance." He concludes that "Jesus' wisdom incorporated the pungent invitation to insight and the daring to be different that characterized the Cynic approach to life."[26]

Seeing Jesus as a Cynic can leads to unrestrained and extreme exaggerations, of course. Professor Lief Vaage of Emmanuel College, Toronto, calls Jesus a party animal, "a bit of a hellion and wanderer on the wild, even illicit, side of things—the original Galilean version of the 1950s rebel James Dean!" Vaage takes the picture painted of Jesus in the Gospels to be that of a man who ate and drank "frequently enough and in sufficient quantity to become notorious for his generous consumption."[27]

To this, James M. Robinson (with whom Vaage studied) levels a stinging rebuke. Jesus was no alcoholic, who would "stumble out of a banquet, stagger down the street in a stupor and whose disciples would leave him laying in the gutter to sleep it off." The problem with presenting Jesus as a Cynic, Robinson argues, "is that it has been a headline-grabbing, sensationalist kind of scholarship. And I think it is a pity."[28]

Of course, there are more temperate views than Vaage's. New Testament scholar Marcus Borg sees Jesus as a charismatic leader, founder of a renewal movement within Judaism, prophet and sage. By eating and drinking with tax collectors and sinners, Jesus challenged "conventional wisdom," the "way of life" or ethos upon which his culture and society was based. This was a prophetic action that called his people to change, inviting them to see differently. Conventional wisdom viewed tax collectors and sinners as outcasts, but God's wisdom sees them, as Jesus saw them, with compassion and grace. As a sage, Jesus' parables and discourses project this image of God, criticizing the dominant way of life and affirming another.[29]

These images are but a few in a wide range of images of Jesus that scholars have presented in the past ten years or so. New Testament professor Daniel Fraikin of Queen's Theological College notes a similar range of views within the Society of Biblical Literature. He believes such diversity is important if the contemporary mind is to form images of Jesus. "For instance, the image of Jesus as a revolutionary or a liberationist or a critic of society are modern categories and are useful for thinking of Jesus in modern terms." Fraikin cautions us, however, that "they are not categories of interpretation in the New Testament. They didn't think that way. But they are useful for the church because they allow us to talk about Jesus in contemporary terms."

Take the notion of Jesus as a Cynic. This, says Fraikin, is "a good reactive element that allows people to say things about Jesus that they wouldn't have said before. I don't see that as very tragic. People who end up with Jesus as Cynic find it very useful to talk about him that way. It is a response to a religious attitude and perhaps there is need to criticize the church as Jesus was critical of the Judaism of his time."[30]

The development of historical Jesus research in this century has produced at least one fascinating pattern. In the 1920s, the majority of persons researching the historical Jesus were German Protestant scholars. Among Jesus scholars today is a "very powerful contingent" of Roman Catholics, who are as fascinated by the historical Jesus as were their Protestant predecessors.[31]

Prior to the twentieth century, biblical criticism had little impact on Roman Catholic studies, and the critical tradition of German Protestantism was looked upon with suspicion. In 1902 Pope Leo XIII (1810-1903), a progressive thinker of his time, established the Pontifical Biblical Commission, which encouraged the new methods of biblical criticism. However, his successor Pope Pius X (1903-1914) condemned the Modernist movement, which aimed at bringing the tradition of Catholic belief into closer relation with modern ideas. This produced a negative reaction to scriptural scholarship that lasted for many years.

It was Pius XII, called by many Roman Catholic scholars "the patron of Catholic biblical studies," who inaugurated "the greatest renewal of interest in the Bible that the Roman Catholic Church has ever seen."[32] His 1943 encyclical *Divino Afflante Spiritu*, in which he encouraged Catholic scholars to use the modern tools of biblical research, is considered the "Magna Carta" of biblical studies. The 1965 Vatican II issued the dogmatic constitution *De Revelatione* (Concerning Revelation), which continued in the line of Pius XII and gave official Church blessing to further progress in biblical research.

Among today's high-profile Catholic scholars are John Dominic Crossan and John Meier. They share similar backgrounds but have reached entirely different views of the historical Jesus, which destroys any notion that Catholic scholars are united in a common view of

Jesus. Both are eminent Roman Catholics engaged in Jesus' research. Both trained for the priesthood in Roman Catholic seminaries. And there the similarities end.

Crossan, who has left the priesthood, breaks with tradition in gathering information for his picture of the historical Jesus. He has expanded the common data base of the canonical Gospels to include extra-canonical works, such as The Gospel of Thomas, because he believes that the "retention, development and creation of Jesus materials are found alike both intracononical and extracanonical";[33] that is, within and without the books recognized by the church as orthodox.

Recent sociological investigations into the Mediterranean world, and archaeological discoveries concerning the Hellenistic character of Galilee have also influenced Crossan's picture of Jesus.[34] So Jesus ends up as a Mediterranean peasant who must be seen in the context of his own society. The kingdom that Jesus spoke of was not the imminent end-of-time intervention of God who would right the evils of this world. Rather, according to Crossan, God's kingdom had already arrived and was expressed in the radical egalitarianism of a peasant society.[35]

Unlike Crossan, Meier holds to the canonical Gospels as the major source of our information about the historical Jesus. However, he readily admits that they are "also the major problem." The Gospels are not primarily works of history in the modern sense. From start to finish, their presentation "is formed by their faith that the crucified Jesus was raised from the dead and will come to judge the world." As well, they give us no information about the historical sequence of the events in Jesus' life. Nevertheless, Meier believes that they are the major source scholars must use to reconstruct the historical Jesus. Other writings, such as the Gospel of Peter or the Gospel of Thomas, are dependent upon the Synoptic Gospels and cannot be used as independent sources for the historical Jesus.[36]

Meier envisions a more Jewish Jesus. He believes that "the very fact that Jesus submitted to John the Baptist's baptism, a fact increasingly played down by the embarrassed evangelists, indicated that Jesus basically accepted John the Baptist's mission and message." Taking aim at Crossan and others who see Jesus as more a Hellenistic sage or Cynic, Meier argues that, at the very least, Jesus behaved as an end-of-time prophet and "prophet," he says, "is an adequate category to explain the full phenomenon of Jesus."[37]

Daniel Fraikin, professor of New Testament at Queen's Theological College, finds the disparate views of Jesus both stimulating and exciting, "the more, the merrier, so to speak. It is the variety that saves us from dogmatism."[38] In Fraikin's view, talking about Jesus outside of a dogmatic, faith context gives Christians a common, universal language with which to dialogue with non-Christians. Christians can't live only in their own conceptual world; they must converse with their contemporaries in secular terms.

The emergence of the image of the historical Jesus as sage or Cynic, however, opens up a theological can of worms. It rests, in part, upon scholar's use of Gospel of Thomas and the reconstructed "Q." However, both documents are unique in that they do not contain a Passion narrative or Resurrection appearance stories. Therefore, they "challenge the assumption that the early church was unanimous in making Jesus' death and resurrection the fulcrum of Christian faith. Both documents presuppose that Jesus' significance lay in his words, and in his words alone."[39] This view is at odds with the tradition that Paul says he received and passed on; namely, that Christ died for our sins according to the Scriptures, that he was buried and raised from the dead according to the Scriptures.[40]

The picture of Jesus as a Cynic, which comes out of the Jesus Seminar and has been popularized by Crossan, Mack, and other scholars, represents Jesus "as one whose disciples had no interest in any redemptive consequence of his death and no interest in his resurrection."[41] This makes even mainstream Christians very uncomfortable and conservative Christians, more so. For is not the belief that after Jesus was crucified he rose from the dead the very foundation upon which the whole edifice of orthodox Christianity is constructed? If you take that away, does the whole edifice come tumbling down?

The Empty Tomb 7

onsider this scenario: After the crucifixion, Jesus' body was placed in the tomb of Joseph of Arimathea. It was then stolen by Simon the Zealot, a follower of Jesus and a member of a radical anti-Roman group, in the hope that popular belief in Jesus' resurrection would help spark a general uprising against the Romans. After killing the guard and rolling away the stone from the tomb's entrance, Simon and three other Zealots carried off Jesus' body and put it into Simon's family tomb. The body was later removed to a cave near Qumran, where the Dead Sea Scrolls were discovered. Almost two thousand years later, an archaeologist finds the bones and a manuscript that appears to authenticate that the bones are indeed those of the crucified Jesus.

The above is the fictitious framework upon which Toronto author Charles Templeton built his novel, *Act of God?* But what if it were true? Would Christianity survive the discovery of Jesus' bones? What would happen to the faith of millions of Christians? Like other writers who have explored the same subject, Templeton has long been intrigued by the story of Jesus' resurrection. A one-time, high-profile, fundamentalist evangelist, Templeton switched from committed Christianity and aggressive evangelism to agnosticism without losing his fascination with Jesus, the man who died on a cross and is said to have risen from the dead. Like others before him, Templeton asked "What if?"

The resurrection of Jesus is one of the most problematic tenets of Christian faith. For many scholars, it presents the most challenging question in the whole academic search for the historical Jesus. Based primarily on Gospel stories of an empty tomb and reports of Jesus' post-resurrection appearances in Jerusalem and Galilee, the resurrection poses a major stumbling block to historical study. Scholars note that the Gospels contain different post-resurrection narratives that take place in different locations, and that there is no agreement as to where Jesus was or what he said after the resurrection. No one seems, at first, to recognize him. Mary Magdalene thinks he is a gardener. And Mark does not offer a concrete description of Jesus' risen body, as the later Gospels do.

If these vague and conflicting Gospel accounts are indeed the only bits of evidence, the case for Jesus' resurrection would not hold water in a court of law, says scholar and author Wilton Barnhardt.[1] To the detractors of Christianity—the pagan Celsus, the Gnostics, Jewish rabbis, the pagan emperor Julian the Apostate, and others—the testimony of the four Gospels has made the task of undermining the resurrection "a simple chore." By definition, then, historical analysis can neither demonstrate nor deny that Jesus' resurrection occurred. It can deal only with belief in the resurrection and the consequences for believers.

Of course, for millions of believers the resurrection is much more than a mere academic exercise, for it is at the very core of their belief. "That Christ died for our sins in accordance with the scriptures, that he was buried, that he was raised on the third day in accordance with the scriptures, and that he appeared to Cephas, then to the twelve," is, for many Christians, as valid today as it was in the time of the Apostle Paul (Cf. 1 Cor. 15:3-5). Remove that belief and, in Paul's words, their faith would indeed be futile and in vain. Yet, even for many ordinary faithful Christians, this article of faith begs for interpretation.

It is argued that without the resurrection there would have been no Christianity. As Jewish scholar Paul Klausner states in *Jesus of Nazareth*, "the tragedy had an 'epilogue': Christianity, would, otherwise, never have been possible."[2] Because the four canonical Gospels provide no narratives of the resurrection itself, it is the dividing line separating the Jesus of history and the Christ of faith.

The rationale for Jesus' miraculous resurrection is that the natural laws that bind humankind were overturned, thus proving his divinity. Without the resurrection, there is no "clinching evidence" that Jesus was more than a great teacher, says Michael Green, advisor on evangelism to the Church of England's Archbishop of Canterbury. "If it [the resurrection] is true, it sets Jesus apart once and for all as the unique Son of God. The worldwide movement that we know as Christianity was launched by the Resurrection." Without the resurrection, adds noted biblical scholar Ben Meyer, Christianity does not make much sense. "Christianity might survive in some kind of crippled form. I do think this is one of those crucial questions."[3]

Belief in the risen Lord is based on accounts of the empty tomb, on Jesus' post-resurrection appearances, and on the dramatic change in the morale of his followers, which motivated them to regroup and to organize the Christian church. For whatever reason, Jesus' disciples were convinced of his resurrection. It is argued that without such a conviction, it is impossible to explain Christianity's survival. That the discovery of the empty tomb was made by women, who by Jewish law were incapable of bearing witness, is often cited as another reason for accepting the resurrection's validity.

As has been noted earlier, the Roman historian Tacitus tells us that "Christus" had been put to death by the "procurator Pontius Pilate in the reign of Tiberius." Add to this the four Gospel accounts of Jesus' crucifixion, and, suggests historian Michael Arnheim—who finds untenable all the claims made for Jesus in Christian creed—we can confidently assert that Jesus not only existed but that he met his death by execution. This execution, he says, was clearly the cause of such acute embarrassment to his followers that it is impossible to believe that it could have been invented by any of them. While Arnheim has no difficulty accepting the historical fact of Jesus' execution, he calls the resurrection a myth required in order to make it possible to believe that Jesus was the Messiah, because a failed and executed Messiah was seen as a contradiction in terms.[4]

Without the resurrection, Jesus would be just a man who had died on the cross. And this would pose serious doctrinal problems for a religion whose central figure is also viewed as divine. As Elaine Pagels writes, the Christian church was born with the proclamation that Jesus Christ rose from the dead, which may be the fundamental element of Christian faith. It's certainly the most radical. Other religions celebrate cycles of birth and death, but it is Christianity that insists that "in one unique historical moment, the cycle was reversed, and a dead man came back to life!"

As Pagels notes, by the second century the Christian writer Tertullian was defining the orthodox position on Jesus' resurrection, leaving no room for doubt. He was not speaking about the immortality of the soul, or in metaphors. What was raised, he said, was flesh, "suffused with blood, built up with bones, interwoven with nerves, entwined with veins...."

Pagels points out that the New Testament accounts of the resurrection could support a range of interpretations. Why then, did Tertullian and other second-century orthodox Christians insist on a literal view of the resurrection and reject others as heretical? Pagels suggests it had as much to do with politics as with religion. Diverse forms of Christianity flourished in the early years of the Christian movement when "hundreds of rival teachers all claimed to teach the 'true doctrine of Christ' and denounced one another as frauds." What was at stake was the leadership of the church and the right to represent "the authentic tradition." Hence the insistence that only one version was authentic and all others heretical "legitimized the authority of certain men who claimed to exercise exclusive church leadership as the successors of the apostle Peter."[5]

Catholic theologian Marianne Sawicki writes that, by the time Mark's Gospel was being written, about forty years after Jesus' death, there were already many "historical Jesuses" based on multiple reconstructions of the facts of Jesus' life and death. And today, like Mark and his contemporaries, "we have several options for how to handle the historical facts" about Jesus' death. Sawicki says that in Mark's day, nobody doubted that Jesus had died a brutal death at the hands of the Romans. The question was, did that death have any significance and value? Different answers were possible, and in fact "found support within the diverse, early Jesus movements."[6]

What makes Jesus significant, says Bart Ehrman, professor of Religion at the University of North Carolina, is that his followers said that God had raised him from the dead, and they convinced other people of that belief. So Christianity began as a religion that subscribed to the death and resurrection of Jesus, rather than being rooted in Jesus' message that the kingdom of God was at hand. In other words, if Jesus' followers had not proclaimed his death and resurrection, we would not have Christianity.[7]

By affirming Jesus' divinity, the early Christian movement moved significantly away from the Jewish notion of the Messiah, says John. L. Collins, professor of Hebrew Bible at Chicago Divinity School. "Christian claims for the divinity of Jesus eventually went beyond anything we find in the Jewish texts. In so far as we know, Jesus of Nazareth was the only historical figure who was eventually identified with Daniel's Son of Man." This title, some scholars suggest, is non-Jewish in origin, coming perhaps from Iranian mythology and denoting a being "chosen by the Lord," the righteous one who reveals all hidden treasures. Although some scholars contend that the title was used by Jesus himself as it is used only by him in the Gospels, many say it was applied to Jesus by primitive Christianity.

The crucifixion of Jesus, says Collins, led to a searching of the Scriptures and to a new, creative examination of biblical references to messianic prophecy, resulting in a "deliberate attempt to claim more for Jesus than had been claimed for any other agent of God."[8]

Divine and human? Human, but not divine? Divine, but not human? Bitter theological disputes about these questions were the growing pains of early Christianity, and they continued to beset a faith trying to explain itself to the world. But in the modern era, Robert Funk suggests, it is the question of Jesus' divinity that mainly fuels public controversies and is made the test of correct belief, particularly on the part of fundamentalists. While it is unlikely that people today would be charged with heresy for questioning that Jesus was human, it was different in the past. One of the earliest heresies in the Christian movement, Funk notes, did deny Jesus' humanity. It was called Docetism—the view that Jesus only appeared to be human, but was in fact a divine figure in disguise.[9]

Historian J. N. D. Kelly says that this tendency to eliminate Christ's humanity "was a factor to be reckoned with from apostolic times onwards" and was not confined to a specific geographical location. Docetism appears to have it roots in the Greek and Oriental assumption that a divine person cannot suffer, is invulnerable, and is free from the impurity of matter. Justin Martyr, the early church philosopher and apologist, "one of the noblest personalities of early Christian literature,"[10] summed up the doctrine when he wrote, "There are some who declare that Jesus Christ did not come in flesh but only in spirit."[11]

It was against these people that Ignatius, the first-century bishop of Antioch, railed, calling them "godless" for claiming that Christ suffered only in appearance.[12] The implication that Jesus' bodily appearance was an illusion is also found in the apocryphal Gospel of Peter, which states that, while on the cross, Jesus "kept silence, as feeling no pain" (4:1).

On the other hand, the Ebionites, members of a Jewish Christian sect that immigrated to the city of Pella on the east side of the Jordan river in A.D. 66 or 67 and who claimed to be followers of Jesus, considered him a mere man, born without divine intervention to Joseph and Mary "according to the ordinary course of human generation." It was also reported that the Ebionites maintained that Paul was an apostate from the Jewish law, while they themselves observed rigidly the customs enjoined by that law. They were, according to Irenaeus, "so Judaic in their style of life, that they even adore Jerusalem as if it were the house of God." The Ebionites' position on Jesus, that he was a great prophet but not the Son of God, is compatible with Islam's view. This led the French historian Jean Daniélou to speculate on the possibility that Muslims came in contact with Ebionites in Transjordan.[13]

The early Christian apologists who proclaimed that Jesus rose from the dead have their modern counterparts in those who assert that the heart of the Christian faith lies in Jesus' divinity and in New Testament claims that he indeed rose from the dead. Just as there was no room for compromise at the time of Tertullian and other Christian apologists, there is no room for compromise today. Either Jesus was a player in what has been called a divine miracle or the whole Christian story is a fable. The Apostle Paul told early Christians in the city of Corinth that "if Christ has not been raised, your faith is futile and you are still in your sins" (1 Cor. 15:17). And those earliest Christians would have agreed with Paul.

William Lane Craig, a conservative Christian scholar, argues that without the historical resurrection Jesus would have been at best just another prophet who met with the same unfortunate fate as others before him, "and faith in him as Messiah, Lord, or Son of God would have been stupid." It would be no use trying to save the situation by interpreting the resurrection as a symbol. The cold, hard facts would remain: "Jesus was dead, and that's it."[14]

Conservative Christians are fond of quoting C. S. Lewis (1898-1963), the Oxford scholar and one of the greatest Christian apologists of this century. For Lewis, Christians had to make a choice. "Either this man was, and is the Son of God: or else a madman or something worse. Let us not come up with any patronizing nonsense about His being a great human teacher. He has not left that open to us. He did not intend to."[15]

However, Lewis' biographer, A. N. Wilson, upbraids him for his argument that only two views of Jesus are possible—Son of God or raving lunatic. Wilson points out that different books of the New Testament have different ways of "describing the indescribable"; that is, the nature of Christ. He says that nowhere in existence is there a set of records that could prove Christ was either a lunatic, or precisely what he said he was, the Son of God. Paul's letters and the Book of Revelation contain "many high and mystical expressions of belief about Christ," but they cannot be described as records of the kind that would compel rational belief. If they were, he suggests that the world would simply be divided into a majority of believing Christians and a small handful of people who were either too stupid or too wicked to accept something obvious and clear-cut. Rather than being clear-cut, Wilson argues that Jesus' nature was the subject of ceaseless disputes among the most learned doctors of the church for the first three centuries of Christendom. The dispute continues today.[16]

Many of today's scholars oppose the literal interpretation of the resurrection, arguing that it was not physical but metaphorical. The Gospel writers, says Jackson Carroll of Duke University, were talking not about the resurrection of the flesh but the resurrection of "Christ's selfhood," his essence. The authors of the New Testament "had experiences with an extraordinary person and extraordinary events, and they were trying to find a way to talk about all that.... They weren't writing scientific history, they were writing faith history."[17]

Many scholars believe that, despite what the Gospels say, Jesus never presented himself as divine during his lifetime. Nor did he present himself as Messiah. It is argued that such titles as Son of Man, Son of God, the Christ, and the Word were applied to him by believing Christians after the resurrection. And these titles are still open to interpretation. The differing New Testament accounts of Jesus' post-resurrection appearances to his Apostles can be problematic for Christians who take the resurrection as factual reports.

And there are those last words of Jesus on the cross. Yale University's David Bartlett says that despite attempts of "harmonizers and oratorio librettists to concoct something like the Seven Last Words," Jesus' words from the cross in each Gospel provide a perspective on each evangelist's particular theological understanding of the crucifixion. For Mark, Jesus is the abandoned Son of God, the suffering one. For Matthew, Jesus is the Messiah who resists the temptation to evade his destiny. For Luke, Jesus is the innocent and faithful one whose courageous and merciful death foreshadows the deaths of Christian martyrs. For John, Jesus dies triumphantly; his death is also his exaltation. Suppose (and it is highly unlikely according to Bartlett) that we find documentary evidence that supports one of these versions of Jesus' last words as being historically more accurate that the others. What would change in our theological understanding of the crucifixion? "Nothing," is Bartlett's answer. "Do we revise our lectionaries so that on each Passion Sunday or Good Friday we preach only on the 'authentic' version of the Last Words? Of course not. The new information might be exceedingly interesting, but it would not be normative for faith, preaching or dogma."[18]

In 1963, the controversial Anglican Bishop of Woolwich John Robinson also noted that, while Jesus' divinity is central to the Christian message, it is also the point where resistance to reinterpretation is greatest and where orthodoxy has its heaviest investment in traditional interpretations. Robinson argued that the New Testament cannot substantiate a supernaturalist view of Christ. "The New Testament says that Jesus was the Word of God, it says that God was in Christ, it says that Jesus is the Son of God; but it does not say that Jesus was God, simply like that."[19]

When, then, did Jesus become God? When, and why, did the belief that he was divine come about? We can immediately point to Paul's epistles as starting points. In his letter to the Christian community in Rome, which contained many Jewish-Christians, Paul writes that Jesus was declared the Son of God by "the resurrection of the dead" (Rom. 1:4). German biblical scholar Hans Conzelmann argues that, while Paul believed in Jesus' divinity, the sources from which he drew his belief viewed Jesus "not as a supernatural being but as a man with a particular status."[20]

Joseph Fitzmyer, a Jesuit priest, points out that in the Jewish world the central idea underlying the use of "Son of God" was that of a person who was divinely elected for a God-given task and obeyed such a vocation. So the title Son of God in Paul's Roman letter is being used in this sense. This could indicate that Jesus was considered divine by his followers only after the resurrection.[21]

But it is obvious from Paul's letter to the Christians in Corinth that he is dealing with some who have difficulty with the idea of resurrection. In an often quoted passage, Paul lays it on the line, spelling out what is probably the earliest preserved credal statement. Reminding the Christians of Corinth that he is handing on to them what he has received—"that Christ died for our sins in accordance with the scriptures, and that he was buried, and that he was raised on the third day" (1 Cor. 15:3-5)—Paul asks how can some of them say there is no resurrection of the dead?

On this point Raymond E. Brown points out that in a pre-Gospel period, as attested by Paul and the sermons in Acts, the resurrection was the chief moment associated with the divine proclamation of the identity of Jesus. Says Brown, "When God raised Jesus from the dead and/or elevated Jesus to his right hand, God made or proclaimed him Lord, Messiah, and Son of God."

The "progressive steps" in Jesus' divinity has also been noted by scholars. By the time the first Gospel was written, the moment when Jesus became divine had moved dramatically back to the time of his baptism by John the Baptist when, according to Mark, a voice came from heaven telling Jesus that "You are my Son, the Beloved" (1:11). In the Gospels of Matthew and Luke, Jesus' divinity is pushed back to his conception, and his identity becomes apparent to his disciples during his ministry. Matthew has the disciples worshipping Jesus as the Son of God (Matt. 14:33), while Peter professes him as the Son of the Living God (Matt. 16:16). By the time of John, Jesus' divinity has been placed prior to creation as a pre-existent divine figure. John puts it this way: "In the beginning was the Word [Jesus], and the Word was with God, and the Word was God."[22]

Although the Word is described as being with God before creation, John shows no interest in philosophical speculation about the relationship of the Father to the Son, a relationship that would later occupy the minds of theologians and church councils. Scholars are at odds about the background of John's use of the term "the Word." The Jewish historian Philo used it in an attempt to bring together the Greek and Hebrew worlds of thought but he never attributed to the Word a personality or a pre-existence. Nevertheless, Raymond Brown contends that the description of the Word in the prologue to John's Gospel is closer to biblical and Jewish thought than to anything Hellenistic. The word of the God that came to the prophets of the Old Testament "has become personal in Jesus who is the embodiment of divine revelation."[23]

Religion professor Larry Hurtado argues that belief in Jesus' divinity began early—possibly as early as within the first decade after Jesus' death. He tends to side with the German theologian Martin Hengel, who argued in his book *The Son of God* that, when it comes to Christological development, more happened within Christianity's first fifteen years than in the next seven hundred. By the year A.D. 40, Jesus is beginning to function as a kind of quasi-divine or divine figure for at least some Christian groups. And there was nothing new about the Gospel writers cloaking Jesus in such honorific titles as Son of God. Such titles were common in Jewish tradition, as was the notion of a heavenly figure who will appear at the end of time and act as a sort of divine agent on behalf of the elect. But the line was drawn at worshipping such a figure. "At the level of rhetoric, almost all the honorific titles given to Jesus in the New Testament paralleled here or there with this or that principal agent figure in non-Christian or pre-Christian Jewish tradition," Hurtado says. "What cannot be paralleled is the way in which at a very early point, Jesus becomes an object of cultic devotion."[24]

There is nothing like a challenge to the resurrection to draw the wagons of orthodoxy into a circle. When what is considered to be fundamental to Christianity is threatened, orthodox Christianity responds with vigour and with anger. It is hardly surprising that Thomas Woolston (1669-1733), an Anglican priest and a Cambridge University fellow, lost his job when he railed against free gifts to the clergy and declared Jesus' resurrection an elaborate cheat got up by the disciples to further their own ambitions.[25]

More recently, in 1986 the Church of England issued a statement reaffirming belief in Jesus' virgin birth and resurrection after the Church's fourth-ranking cleric publicly expressed doubts about the virgin birth and said he favoured a natural explanation for the empty tomb. "Disciples might have pinched the body" was how one English newspaper headlined a story about David Jenkins, then Bishop of Durham, who is reported to have called the resurrection a "conjuring trick with bones." In an Easter message, Jenkins, a former professor of theology at Leeds University, said he did not believe that Jesus Christ literally rose from the dead. To insist on literal language as being the only way of bearing witness to God is to get stuck in something very close to magic and superstition and to be "in great danger of encouraging many unbelievers in their conviction that we religious people deal in fairy tales." What sort of God are we portraying and believing in if we insist on "the laser beam" type of miracle as the base of the incarnation and resurrection? "The fact of the resurrection is quite unproveable and unpersuasive, except to those who believe."

Jenkin's statements caused an uproar. He was accused of heresy and blasphemy. However, Jenkins was far from being a lone wolf. A poll of England's thirty-nine bishops revealed that about a third of them shared the bishop's thoughts about this article of faith. *The Economist*, a prestigious weekly publication of news and opinion, didn't. It chided the doubting bishop: "Mr Jenkins is not merely challenging say, the biblical myth of creation, some obscure detail of doctrine or even some weighty tradition—that women cannot be priests, for instance—which the church has built up over the centuries." By publicly expressing his doubts, Jenkins had, *The Economist* said, attacked the very heart of Christianity. Did Jenkins's lips move when he recited the Creed? the news weekly asked. And, if they did, why?[26]

Despite his highly unorthodox views, John Spong, the Episcopal Bishop of Newark, says he can recite the Nicene Creed with conviction but is not bound by "a literal fourth-century interpretation of the words." Spong has described the Gospel narratives of Jesus' resurrection as "late developing, pious legends." There was no tomb, and the body of Jesus was, in all probability, thrown into an unmarked, common grave used for criminals, covered over and forgotten. And yet, Spong states that the resurrection is so central to Christianity that without it there would be no Christianity. He distinguishes, however, between the narratives of the disciples that purport to describe the resurrection and the actual resurrection. Isolate Paul from the rest of the New Testament, he suggests, and just read him "without your mind being corrupted by the later images of the Gospel," and you will discover that even Paul does not believe that the resurrection was a physical event. "For Paul, it was not being raised from the grave back into the life of the world. It was being raised from death into God."[27]

In 1994, Gerd Lüdemann's *The Resurrection of Jesus: History, Experience, Theology* was dismissed with a terse "nonsense" by Vienna's Roman Catholic Cardinal Koenig. Even some of Lüdemann's academic colleagues, as well as lay people, condemned the book as "scholarly worthless" and "pure fantasy." Lüdemann, a faculty member at the University of Göttingen, found himself in the middle of a theological minefield after writing that Jesus' body remained in the grave, that nothing happened on the "third day," and that Jesus' post-crucifixion appearances were nothing more than visions by the disciples.

"Can we still be Christians?" asked the influential German weekly newsmagazine *Der Spiegel* at the height of the controversy in March 1994. "Is there no Easter?" asked an evangelical Lutheran newspaper. The public outcry appears to have spooked the renowned publishing house of Vandenhoeck and Ruprecht, which has a long history of publishing books by eminent theologians, such as Rudolf Bultmann. According to a *Der Spiegel* report, the publisher distanced itself from the book even before it reached the distributors, sold only the already printed sample copies, and told Lüdemann to find another publisher.

The potential for much the same negative reaction was very much on the minds of Jesus Seminar organizers as they prepared for their April 1995 meeting. In discussing, and voting, on Gospel accounts of Jesus' resurrection, the Jesus Seminar cautioned the faint-hearted that it would be "drilling close to the nerve of the Christian faith." Just in time for Easter, when interest in the Jesus' passion and resurrection is at its height, the Seminar concluded that claims of Jesus' resurrection are statements of faith and not reports of a historical event or events. The empty tomb story, the Seminar voted, is a legend that developed three or four decades after Jesus' death, probably in response to the rumour that Jesus' followers had stolen the body.

The Seminar also noted that the visionary experiences of Jesus are variously reported to have gone on for months, perhaps even years. The risen Christ's appearance to Paul as a blinding light and a voice must have taken place three or four years after the crucifixion, not in the forty days following Easter. In his Gospel, Luke reports that Jesus ascended to heaven on Easter Sunday evening, but then has Jesus tarry on earth for forty days in the opening paragraphs of the book of Acts. The Seminar also pointed out that *Secret James*, a book of the Nag Hammadi Library, has Jesus continuing his instructions to his disciples for 550 days, while *Pistis Sophia*, a collection of writings emanating from Egypt in the third century, represents Jesus as prolonging his instruction of certain followers for eleven years. "Reported sightings of Jesus continue, even into twentieth-century America," the Seminar said. "All of these claims make it difficult to say how long Easter lasted."[28] The reaction to these conclusions was predictable.

Like other conservative Christians, Kevin Quast, a teacher of New Testament at the conservative Ontario Theological Seminary, dismisses such conclusions as "unfounded theological suppositions." While he acknowledges that there are few places in the Gospels where Jesus claimed directly that he was God, "he accepts titles and worship that belong only to God." Even the angry reaction of his enemies "show that they understood his claims and they were scandalized by them. That is why he was crucified."

For Quast, this is a strong point. It enables him to carry forward his argument that what Paul said in First Corinthians, chapter 15, could not be clearer and to deny the bodily resurrection of Jesus is "to strip the Christianity of its essential message." Rather than making the Gospels easier to accept, those Christians who deny the physical resurrection empty "the Christian faith and hold up Christians to ridicule." The very essence of Christianity is Jesus' nature and is summed up, for Quast, in a trust and a faith in Jesus as the Son of God who died and rose again on our behalf. And "if we don't believe that then, personally, we don't have a Christian faith."

Quast considers himself "left of centre from the evangelical perspective" with a fundamental commitment to the authority of scripture. He says the discovery of Jesus' body would force him to give up his Christian faith: "If it were proven without a shadow of a doubt that they were the bones of Christ, my integrity would not allow me to remain a Christian. If Christ did not rise from the dead, if the historical event upon which all Christian doctrine is built did not happen, I would not be able to be a Christian according to the witness of the Bible."[29]

The Jesus Seminar can reach as many conclusions as it likes, but the resurrection remains a bedrock of Christianity for conservative Christians such as Graham Scott, a United Church minister and editor of *Theological Digest* and *Outlook*. And those who deny it as such "have left the Christian faith."[30] However, Dominic Crossan and other liberal scholars who affirm their Christian faith take issue with such a position. Crossan says that even the discovery of Jesus' bones would not destroy his faith. "What happens to bodies. I leave to God," he says.

Crossan has suggested that rather than having been put reverently in a tomb, Jesus' body was left to the mercy of scavenging dogs or other animals. Not surprisingly, many Christians take loud exception to this point of view. "Since he does not accept the historicity of the discovery of the empty tomb, not to speak of the resurrection, Crossan merely surmises that Jesus' corpse was laid in a graveyard reserved for executed criminals," says William Craig. Rather than relying on the evidence that "prompts most scholars to accept the historicity of Jesus' entombment," Craig says Crossan seeks to undercut the credibility of the Gospel accounts of Jesus' burial and resurrection by means of a general analysis of the Gospel texts and traditions that is "so bizarre and contrived that the overwhelming majority of the New Testament critics find it wholly implausible, idiosyncratic speculation."[31]

Presbyterian minister James Dickey, former editor of *The Presbyterian Record*, believes firmly in the resurrection "in some form" without worrying too much about the specific details. He says finding Jesus' body would not deny what those earlier followers experienced. "And they experienced something, and it was not in their own heads. It got these frightened people, virtually impotent to do anything, moving." From that event came the church with "all its universality, and all its stupidity as well, and it has survived for two thousand years." Something happened to turn these people around: "They gained nothing. They lost their lives in many cases. They did not make money. All the traditional motives for a hoax do not hold up."

Dickey says the Gospel language dealing with the resurrection is somewhat "strange," betraying confusion on the part of those who saw Jesus after his crucifixion. However, he suggests that rather than diminishing the Gospels' accounts, this adds weight to them: "If it was cooked, they would be a lot more definite. But there is this shock, this puzzlement. Something happened, and it was outside the normal run of human experience."[32]

One can only imagine the newspaper headlines and the television bulletins if the bones of Jesus were reported to be found. If we assume there was some scientifically credible proof, the news would have a profound affect on Christians. Some would be so devastated that they would abandon or lose their faith, as many did when they read Darwin. Others would re-examine and adjust their theology. No doubt some would refuse to believe the evidence, declaring it part of a plot by Satan to destroy Christianity, or another example of media sensationalism made for a tabloid's lurid headline.

Of course, not every Christian would panic. "It would certainly eliminate certain theological possibilities," says Larry Hurtado. "It would mean that when you say, Jesus is risen from the dead, you don't mean that it affected his physical remains. You mean some other kind of mystical, or spiritual, or one of the other three or four options that are out there. At present, all the options remain theologically open. Finding the body of Jesus would foreclose one of those options. But it would not necessarily foreclose all options."[33]

What's Left for Sunday? 8

The local pastor was listening intently to what was being said and was growing more agitated by the minute. Finally, he'd had enough and spoke out. "You guys say, 'this didn't happen and that didn't happen. What I want to know is, what do I have left to tell my people? What are you leaving me with to talk about on Sunday?"

The occasion was a public forum in Muncie, Indiana, featuring a telecast of some of the Jesus Seminar's leading lights. The questioning pastor was from a local church and, as university professor Chris Shea recalls, he appeared more perplexed than angry: "He argued, quite forcefully really, that everybody who had ever been in a seminary knew much of this stuff, but he didn't see what good it was doing for Christians in the community. The argument was quite vigorous. He was an honest man and he was perplexed ... he didn't want to think of himself as being an Elmer Gantry."[1]

As they watch Jesus and traditional Christianity being slowly pared away, there are many who sympathize with that Muncie pastor. Just what will be left when the avant-garde scholars finish their whittling? Andrew Greeley, Roman Catholic priest and a prolific author known to all browsers of popular paperbacks, says there will still be plenty left to provide spiritual nourishment. He advises people to keep the faith; to hang on to the stories. Even when one gets down to the bare minimum of sayings and parables, he says the man encountered is still a fascinating mystery. "Even if all one has is the handful of quotes and stories that Robert Funk, the *doyen* of the [Jesus] seminar, admits in his books, Jesus is still a challenge, still an extraordinary man with special insight, still a person with a vision that no one ever had before or since."

While recognizing historical reconstruction as an essential scholarly work, Greeley says it runs the risk of tearing apart the stories in search of historical truth. There are "some folk, pious and reasonably well-educated," who feel the early church distorted Jesus, lost sight of his message, and that one must get beyond the Gospels and back to Jesus himself to find out what he really said. That, suggests Greeley, will lead you up a blind alley. "A friend of mine tried it once and gave it up because, as he said, when he finally found the 'historical Jesus', there was hardly anyone there."[2]

The idea of finding "hardly anyone there" worries any believer, especially those who think of themselves as conservative Christians. Some denounce what they see as liberal theological assaults on their beliefs. Others fight back from the pulpit, in the classrooms of conservative seminaries, or through the pages of conservative publications, as they ponder how best to confront the Jesus Seminar and the wider body of liberal scholarship.

Back in 1963, Bishop John Robinson wrote in his controversial book, *Honest to God* that we stood on the brink of a period in which it was going to become increasingly difficult to know what the true defence of Christian truth required. He correctly foresaw a growing gulf between the "traditional orthodox supernaturalism" in which Christianity has been framed and a fresh understanding that would be meaningful in an increasingly secular society. He was not sanguine about bridging the gulf in the near future. Predicting a widening gap between liberal and conservative Christianity, Robinson saw increasing polarization, both inside and outside the church, between those "whose basic recipe is the mixture as before" and those "who feel compelled above all to be honest wherever it may lead them."[3]

History appears to have come down on Robinson's side. As we approach the twenty-first century, the gulf has widened, giving rise to fears of even greater alienation and deeper polarization. Conservative scholars accuse their liberal colleagues of holding views that border on the heretical. Conservative theologians say mainstream theological colleges are being infiltrated by ideas uncomfortably close to those held by the Jesus Seminar. Confused, fearful, and angry, many Christians believe that Christianity is being gutted.

The currents of theological arguments, the new emphasis on the relativism of the Bible, and the challenge to accepted concepts of the nature of Christ and his relation to the Godhead, all amount, it is argued, to a severe departure from the received understanding of Christianity and to the faith of most believers.

As has been said before, the stakes are high. If it were proved conclusively that Julius Caesar never lived, the world would not fall apart. But it were proved conclusively that Jesus of Nazareth never lived, the world, as some have suggested, would never be the same.[4] With this in mind, it is not unreasonable to expect the issue to become even more polarized. Robert Bater, a biblical scholar and United Church minister, expects the battle over Jesus' nature to be as divisive for late twentieth- and early twenty-first-century Christians as was the theological battle over evolution in the early part of this century. As with the evolution controversy, lines are being drawn in the sand as both sides marshal their forces. This is an interesting and telling comparison; in both cases there seems to be a deep assumption that spiritual matters are important, that people search for a faith to live by.

According to Bater, "one of the major issues is going to be this: does theology, all our theological beliefs and structures that are centuries old, have to come to the bar of history again? The work of the Jesus Seminar and the whole wider group of scholars, new archaeological investigations, such as those of Sepphoris, work on the Nag Hammadi Library and the Dead Sea Scrolls, are certainly going to pose tougher questions about the continuum from Jesus to the Christian Church." And Bater suspects there will be some real tough questions raised as the church grapples with re-examining that continuum. He names two of those questions: the Paul-versus-Jesus controversy and women in the early church.

Take those "superb doctrines" of Paul by which Christians have lived for centuries. How exactly or how necessarily they relate to the Jesus of history is, for Bater, a vital question: "We have not even begun to face the questions at the simplest level. We have always known that there was a problem about the relationship between Paul and Jesus. What would Jesus have thought if he really had a chance to respond to Paul's interpretation and his whole theological edifice? We've always skirted over that lightly."

What would Jesus have thought of Paul's interpretation of the Jewish Law in his letters to the Galatians and to the Romans? Paul proclaimed the end of the Law and said that a person need not follow it to be righteous before God. One need only believe in Jesus Christ. But Jesus himself would certainly have the same opinion of the Law as the Jewish historian Josephus, who said he could imagine nothing "more righteous" than obeying the statutes of the Law.[5] It is improbable that Jesus thought the sacred Jewish Law, given by God to Moses on Mount Sinai, was only a temporary means of salvation and that faith in him would be the only thing necessary.

And then there is the matter of attitudes towards the role of women in the early church and in Jesus' own ministry: the politics implicit in the Gospel of Mary, the struggles between various disciples over the role of Mary. "It isn't just a nice easy continuity," Bater says. "There are some real tough spots there."[6] That Jesus had women among his followers is clear from the Gospels. All the Gospel narratives that describe Jesus' encounters with women portray him as most sympathetic to them. The early church certainly had women in positions of authority and influence; Paul even names some influential women in the greetings at the end of his letters. In the final chapter of his Letter to the Romans, he mentions Phoebe who is a deaconess and sends greetings to Priscilla and her husband Aquila who share the office of instruction with Paul. There is also a passing greeting to a Mary who has laboured hard for the Roman community (Rom. 16).

Nevertheless there are conflicting statements concerning women in the New Testament. Paul's letter to the Corinthian community permits women to pray and to speak to the church at one point but it then imposes silence upon them (Cf. 1 Cor. 11:4; 14:3, 4f.). This ambivalence often leads to Christians quoting Paul in order to deny women a role in the church. The strongly worded exhortation in the letter to Timothy, that women "must listen in silence and be completely submissive," is from a later period and shows a marked change in attitude towards women (1 Tim. 2:11). There is clearly a diminishing of women's roles in the early church.

Gordon Melton, director of the California-based Institute for the Study of American Religion sees the rise of religious diversity in the West as a major factor in the growing polarization between liberal and conservative Christianity. This diversity, he says, has been accompanied theologically by a re-evaluation and a letting go of some claims for uniqueness formerly espoused within the Christian community.[7]

While conservative Christian denominations refuse to budge on the issue of Jesus' divinity, some liberal denominations wrestle with the question of Jesus' uniqueness in a world of competing religious claims. "Welcome to the United Church's next big controversy" is how *The United Church Observer* introduced a March 1991 cover story on how church members see Jesus. The Rev. Walter Farquharson, then Church moderator, dismissed talk of a looming controversy as bordering on the sensational: "The United Church has always been able to encompass in lively tension different expressions of faith. And wherever the church has imposed a rigidity of thought or a rigidity of

practice or a rigidity of experience by which to test truth and orthodoxy, it has moved towards death."

Yet conservative United Church members believe the Church is
moving away from a "classical, orthodox Christianity." Donald Faris,
United Church minister and author, argues that rather than presenting a clear, firm expression of classical Christian beliefs, the United
Church is being deliberately ambiguous about what it believes in order not to offend other faiths: "They are being vague about the authority of Scripture and muddy about the full divinity and the full
humanity of Christ."[8]

The claim that Jesus Christ is unique, the "truth, the way and the
life," is the bedrock of evangelical theology, says Don Posterski, evangelical Christian, author, and researcher. And that claim is non-negotiable: "I would identify the uniqueness of Christ as a non-negotiable
point of preservation for Christian plausibility. Let's be careful about
what we disregard. The danger of the age is we can suffer from a
continual erosion, and whenever we get to the point of surrendering
our point of uniqueness, we are getting close to self-sacrifice." Having said that, Posterski adds that he fears evangelicals, rather than
being "open to what is," will "pull the blinds down attitudinally" leading to further isolation and polarization. "That's maybe because there
is a closed-mindedness on certain issues," he says. "Living in this
modern world, the best counsel is to figure out what your non-
negotiables are, then work to affirm substance in them. You have to
work to find a position of committed clarity on a few things that
allows you to investigate many other things."

Posterski affirms standard evangelical beliefs: the historical existence of Jesus is a fact and "his miraculous intervention in the world
as the long-promised Messiah is certain." Jesus is "in a class by himself, in a world by himself," because "his divine visitation in human
form never happened before in history and will never happen again
in history." That, in a nutshell, is the uniqueness Posterski wants to
hang onto. Anything the Jesus Seminar says, or does, is unlikely to

shake that conviction. "As far as damaging the confidence of con-servative Christians, the Jesus Seminar is not even a marginal threat. I see almost no impact on people in the pews or on evangelical lead-ers. The assumptions of the Seminar are so far away from the as-sumptions of conservative Christians that they are not taken as a se-rious threat."[9]

It is particularly vexing, however, for more than conservatives, when extensive media coverage of Jesus Seminar meetings leads to newspaper headlines such as, "Lord's Prayer Isn't His." The results of the vote on the Lord's Prayer attracted more headlines than any other vote, and news of it appeared as front-page stories in more than one hundred Sunday newspapers. All of this can sow confusion among ordinary Christians, suggests Larry Hurtado of the University of Mani-toba. "They pick up the newspapers and it says that Jesus Seminar scholars say such and such and they don't know what to do with it."

Any historical critical work, any attempt to get inside the early development of Christianity or the historical Jesus, is bound, accord-ing to Hurtado, to have profound implications for Christians. While Christian theologians are equipped to roll with the punches, and to access the evidence in a critical manner, "the person in the pew who hasn't had any kind of advanced philosophical, theological or histori-cal training, is very ill-equipped to assess all this stuff."[10]

But apparently being theologically ill-equipped does not inhibit some people in the pews from asking pointed questions. Raymond Humphries, New Testament scholar at Toronto's Knox College, has noticed that an increasing number of lay people are raising questions about basic Christian beliefs. "Wait a minute, what does that mean? Please tell us what that means," is not an uncommon request from ordinary churchgoers, says Humphries. People want to know the Je-sus behind all the theological language because they are more aware of biblical criticism. And they are beginning to chaff at being left out of the scholarly debate.

On the other hand, Humphries suggests there are fewer people who are biblically literate in Protestant circles: "Our tradition has always been that the Bible was the authority. I grew up in a tradition where people knew their Bible very well and that is getting lost." And it's happening at a time when liberal scholars are challenging the evangelists' presentation of Jesus as "Lord and God" replacing it with a "more unitarian type of presentation of Jesus." The big question for Humphries is how far this liberal presentation will go in the churches.[11]

If the kind of scholarship espoused by the Jesus Seminar were to be taken as standard and become deeply influential, it could deal a blow to traditional Christianity that would be hard to absorb, says biblical scholar Ben Meyer, who holds a "standard Catholic theology of Jesus." But he expects Christianity to weather the storm, as it has in the past: "Ever since 1835-36, when David Strauss published his *Life of Jesus*, there has been a trashing of Gospel literature and I don't think Protestant theology has ever recovered from it." Now along comes the Jesus Seminar with a Jesus who has been stripped of much of his traditional covering. "But it will not make much difference what they do," he says. "They will have no power over this generation or the next. They only have a few leaders and their reduction of what Jesus said to twenty per cent is ideological."

Meyer declined an invitation to join the Jesus Seminar because of ill health. He now wishes he had accepted the invitation in order to "take on some of my friends" and challenge some of their controversial conclusions. Lamenting the lack of solid counter-arguments to Jesus Seminar pronouncements, Meyer calls for a "genuine engagement between the foolishness of the Jesus Seminar and a body of articulate, sane people working with a solid hermeneutics."[12]

Prompted by what it perceives as the Jesus Seminar's growing and unchallenged influence, the Catholic Biblical Society plans to answer Meyer's call. "It's about time we started talking back," says Jesuit Terry Prendergast, biblical scholar and a Toronto assistant bishop. "A lot of people have been influenced by it [the Jesus Seminar]." The Biblical Society plans to set up its own historical Jesus seminar in 1996. "We don't want to get into an adversarial position," adds Prendergast. "What we want to do is say 'here's what we think.' There is no point in getting *ad hominem* or berating them. They say let's have an academic discussion, and we are going to take up that challenge. If biblical scholars don't pay any attention to them, we are in real trouble. We need sound scholarship. The church needs it."[13]

If the Jesus Seminar has done nothing else, it has made people sit up and take notice. And that, states Douglas Hall, one of North America's most noted systematic theologians, in itself serves Christianity well: "What they are doing is probably a counter-balance to something else that is happening in the churches, a kind of neglect of Jesus, a neglect of Christology. It's important for the church to exercise careful scholarship and to ask if this statement or that statement is truly attributable to Jesus. Is it likely he said this, or was it possibly something the later church had him say for certain purposes? That kind of scholarly question has got be asked, always." Such questioning, Hall suggests, will not lead to Christianity's demise, or the death of faith. "It's a bit like what [the renowned theologian Paul] Tillich used to say: 'We can't really allow the faith of the church to be determined by some discovery that may be made in the sands of Egypt.'"[14]

Will the Jesus Seminar "movement" be shortlived? Or is it the early warning rumble of the collapse of traditional Christian belief among many North American churchgoers? There may be some damage, but it's unlikely that twenty centuries of Western culture will be undone "in one smart-alecky grunt of scholarship."[15] In reality, this current intense interest in the historical Jesus is very much a Western, and particularly a North American, phenomenon. For many Christians in Africa and South America, competing with Islam or aggressive evangelical Christian sects, the quest for the historical Jesus is an intellectual luxury they can ill afford.

But it is interesting that religious pluralism poses challenges to mainstream Christian denominations. Take the Roman Catholic

Church in Africa where, despite a rapid growth in membership, the Church is competing with Islam for converts. Many bishops at a 1994 synod challenged the Church to present an "African Christ"—a Christ embodied in African culture, just as Christ was embodied in Greek and Latin cultures.[16]

While mainstream Christian denominations outside North America try to counteract the very effective proselytizing efforts of evangelical sects, many North American conservative Christians express concern at the "creeping liberalism" infiltrating not only the churches but also the places of learning where the next crop of ministers and teachers are being trained. "Academia is very, very rationalistic," says Graham Scott, who also fears the United Church will further shunt Jesus aside in the name of religious pluralism, leading to a split, a "cleavage of the soul" between liberals and conservatives. "But you can never predict what is going to happen," adds Scott. "The Jesus Seminar is too extreme, and it might drive people into faith without intending too. Kierkegaard was so intense that he drove some people into atheism. By way of contrast, Nietzsche was so intense that he drove some people into faith."[17]

Whatever its impact, scholars such as N. Thomas Wright are convinced that the quest for the historical Jesus will occupy centre stage for some time to come. Historical search, he says, deals ultimately with issues that lie in the public domain, not with matters that can only be discussed within the "household of faith." There is plenty of evidence that the quest for the historical Jesus is both as alive and important now as it ever has been.

There is little to suggest that the search for the historical Jesus will run out of steam—at least in the foreseeable future. "If you show up at any Jesus session at the Society for Biblical Literature, the place is packed," Wright notes. "Fifteen years ago it wasn't so. There wasn't much historical Jesus stuff. It was considered off limits." While crediting scholars such as Crossan for helping turn that around, Wright also suggests the historical Jesus search is getting bogged down in agendas: "There are nineteen different types of Christian agendas. People escaping from their fundamentalist background like Bob Funk, people escaping their tight Roman Catholic background like Dominic Crossan, and other people feeling their way back to some sort of faith from nowhere like Marcus Borg. And in the middle of it are typical Anglicans like me, who are just trying to understand what we are doing."

Why all the interest? Its partly due, Wright suggests, to the "huge cultural shifts and transitions going on from modernism to post-modernism" There is a sense of, "Help! help! There must be some roots somewhere—where can we go back to?" Christians who pick up a newspaper and read that a totally different Jesus from their conception is being portrayed in some quarters are asking, "Is its true?" Many "good Christian folk" may wonder if their whole way of life has been based on a mistake.[18] It may be, as Marcus Borg suggests, an indication of a rebirth of religious interest by many people "whose childhood understanding of Jesus and the Bible at some time stopped working but whose religious interest remains."[19]

What waits to be discovered in the burning sands of Egypt or in the land where Jesus trod? Archaeological research, as Neil Asher Silbermann notes, has neither proved nor disproved the historical existence of Jesus, John the Baptist, or the Apostles, but it has provided information on a wide range of early Roman period sites in Judea and Galilee and has documented their changing material culture. And this evidence, says Silbermann, has now become the raw material for a far-reaching historical reassessment of first-century Judean and Galilean life.[20]

How much more information will science be able to reveal about the past? Scientists can now apply DNA typing techniques to the Dead Sea Scrolls and other texts written on goat skin some two thousand years ago. The technique is so precise that it enables scholars to identify not only the species but the herd and individual animals the parchment comes from.[21]

Just as Galileo forced the theologians of his day to at least consider the ramifications of his scientific conclusion, so modern theology is being forced into a new way of thinking to keep up with the scientific discoveries of the late twentieth century. Genetic engineering is but one example where a new theological vocabulary is needed to articulate the relationship between God and modern man. New conflicts dealing with the ethics of life, procreation, and sexuality are replacing traditional doctrinal divisions between the major Christian churches. Traditional Christianity itself is being dismissed as outdated, not by modern-day Voltaires, but by eminent, albeit radical, theologians and clerics.

A leading light in what is referred to as a non-supernatural version of Christianity is Cambridge theology lecturer Don Cupitt, an Anglican priest and former dean of Cambridge's Emmanuel college. Dubbed the "atheist vicar," Cupitt has written what has been called the first textbook of post-Christianity in which he argues that it is dishonest to pretend that the Christian story is true in any sense. As a myth, as a system of signs, it may be useful. But that, he says, is as far as it goes.[22] Cupitt is reported to have quite a wide popular following among young Anglican pastors of "progressive tendencies," who identify themselves with a "free Christianity."[23]

The question might well be asked: is there any room for Jesus in all of this? Scholars such as Steve Humphries-Brooks believes there is. We are nowhere near a scholarly consensus that is going to eliminate so much from Jesus that pastors can't preach on him. And there is unlikely to be a point where it can be said with absolute certainty whether there is a whole lot left, or nothing left, of Jesus after all the historical probing.[24]

So it appears unlikely that radical theologians, the Jesus Seminar, or any other set of scholars will come up with a set of definitive answers or set the criterion for Christian faith. And, indeed, Seminar scholars have said as much. As Marcus Borg says, the Seminar is aware that one cannot actually determine what Jesus said, or did, by a process of voting: "Voting cannot settle historical questions and majorities (even consensus majorities) are sometimes wrong. Moreover, we know that the votes on some of the sayings would likely be quite different ten or twenty years from now, just as votes on some would likely have been different twenty or thirty years ago."[25]

Without much doubt, portraits of Jesus of Nazareth will continue to rely on the artist's creativity and the images people carry with them in their minds. What to do with the man in the scarlet robe was a quandary for Pontius Pilate, and Jesus remains a quandary, a puzzle, for many of today's biblical scholars and theologians.

No doubt, scholars will continue to pump out "Jesus" books, and the value of these books, as Leander Keck suggests, will not be in what they say about Jesus so much as in how they make people think about what is being said. And scholars who think they've come to the end of the quest will still see their own reflections in the well, mentioned by Schweitzer at the turn of this century.[26]

Interestingly enough, all this debate over the historical Jesus is going on at a time when church attendance, in North America at any rate, is falling rapidly. The days of institutional Christianity, says Konrad Raiser, general secretary of the World Council of Churches, seem to be numbered, and once powerful churches appear "powerless in the face of growing social disintegration and the erosion of values."[27] The McDonald's hamburger chain logo is recognized by more people than the Christian cross.[28] For many people, Jesus, if known at all, is no more than the name of a man who died on a cross almost two thousand years ago, and gave his name to a religion.

So why do so many continue to try, often with a sense of urgency, to come up with answers to that question posed so many years ago: "Who do people say that I am'?" Well, for one thing, as church historian Rowan Greer puts it, "it's a good yarn, a good mystery story." Doing ancient history, he says, is like trying to work a jigsaw puzzle with three-quarters of the pieces missing. What you have to do is to examine the pieces that are left, try to figure out in an imaginative way what the other pieces would look like, and then try to fit them together. It's not like a detective story "where the criminal 'fesses up' at the end. You just don't know."[29]

In the long run, we can really only speculate and wonder. It does seem possible, says Dominic Crossan, that the function of the various "Christs" by which Jesus has been interpreted has been to "mute, mitigate or manage his program in ways that would not challenge civilization so basically and so profoundly." In other words, the "real" Jesus might be just too hard to take.

Crossan would like to reopen what he calls the ancient debate between "an incarnational or catholic Christianity"—the belief that Christ was fully human and fully divine—and "an anti-incarnational or Gnostic Christianity, which denied Christ's full humanity. The original question was decided not theologically but politically; not by Christian debate but by Roman power. Given Crossan's backround and reputation, he appears just the man to reopen the debate. His reasoning is that it would force theology finally to answer this question: "What does Jesus have to do with Christ? Does Jesus help us decide between Christs?"[30]

But perhaps most search for the historical Jesus for less profound reasons. Perhaps it is an elusive thing that defies words. In 1617, the Italian composer Claudio Monteverdi wrote a five-part motet to honour the finding of relics—believed to be fragments of the True Cross—during the construction of St. Peter's in Rome. In the Middle Ages, parts of the True Cross were so numerous that it was waggishly said that there were enough of them to rebuild the entire city of Jerusalem. It's doubtful that anyone today believes in the relics' authenticity. It's doubtful whether the relics still exist. And yet, as historian Steward Sutherland reminds us, Monteverdi's beautiful motet has been preserved and is performed regularly. Although the historical belief that inspired its composition is now discredited, "the music is no less delightful, nor at all diminished in quality or value."[31]

The same could be said of the search for the historical Jesus, the man in the scarlet robe.

Notes

Preface

1. Cf. James Charlesworth, *Jesus and the Dead Sea Scrolls* (New York: Doubleday, 1992), 162.
2. John Dominic Crossan, a charter member of the Jesus Seminar, in a *Toronto Star* interview.
3. Paul Verhoeven, interview with Michael McAteer.
4. Louis Cassels, *This Fellow Jesus* (Anderson, Indiana: Warner Press, 1973), 10.

Introduction

1. Cf. Thomas F. Mathews, *The Clash of Gods: A Reinterpretation of Early Christian Art* (Princeton, Pa.: Princeton University Press, 1993), 180.
2. John Dominic Crossan, interview with Michael McAteer.

Chapter 1: The Colour of Truth

1. The Jesus Seminar now operates out of Santa Rosa.
2. From Robert Funk's address to the original Charter Fellows of the Jesus Seminar in March 1985. See *The Five Gospels: The Search for the Authentic Words of Jesus*, new translation and commentary

by Robert W. Funk, Roy H. Hoover, and the Jesus Seminar (New York: Macmillan, 1993), 34.

3. Marcus J. Borg is Hundere Distinguished Professor of Religion at Oregon State University. See *Jesus in Contemporary Scholarship*, (Valley Forge, Pa.: Trinity Press International, 1994), 162.

4. Marcus J. Borg, Jesus Seminar news release, 6 March 1995.

5. John Dominic Crossan, interview with Michael McAteer.

6. Cf. Julian V. Hills, "Tradition, Redaction, and Intertextuality: Miracle Lists in Apocryphal Acts," *Society of Biblical Literature 1990 Seminar Papers*, ed. David J. Lull (Atlanta, Ga.: Scholars Press, 1990), 375-390.

7. Paul Verhoeven, interview with Michael McAteer.

8. Acts 2:19-20; 2 Thess 1:7.

9. Cf. *The Five Gospels*, 35.

10. Cf. Roy Hoover, "The Search for the Authentic Words of Jesus," *The Fourth R*, vol. 7, no. 1 (Jan./Feb. 1994), 3-6.

11. Albert Schweitzer, *The Quest of the Historical Jesus: A Critical Study of its Progress from Reimarius to Werde* (London: Adam & Charles Black, 1948), 399.

12. Robert W. Funk, Bernard Brandon Scott, and James R. Butts, *The Parables of Jesus: Red Letter Edition; A Report of the Jesus Seminar* (Sonoma, Calif.: Polebridge Press, 1988), xii.

13. William Macklin in "Did Jesus Have Speechwriters?" by Thomas Cairns, *The Toronto Star* (Jan. 10, 1994), A15.

14. Cf. Russell Sorto, "Cross Fire," *G.Q.* (June 1994), 118.

15. N. Thomas Wright, interview with Michael Steinhauser.

16. John Meier, professor of New Testament at The Catholic University of America, Washington, D.C., in James D. Davis, *Fort Lauderdale Sun-Sentinel* (Feb. 21, 1992).

17. Cf. Richard Hays, "The Corrected Jesus," *First Things* (May 1994), 43-48.

18. Terrance Prendergast in "Gospel Truth" by Michael McAteer, *The Toronto Star* (July 2, 1994), K12.

19. John Meier, in Davis, *Fort Lauderdale Sun-Sentinel*.
20. Robert Bater, interview with Michael McAteer.
21. Daniel Bogert-O'Brien, in "Gospel of Thomas will be focus of study" by Michael McAteer, *The Toronto Star*, (Oct. 12, 1991), F13.
22. Graham Scott, interview with Michael McAteer.
23. Timothy George, "Why We Believe in the Virgin Birth," *Christianity Today* (Dec. 12, 1994), 18-19. Cf. Justin, *Apology*, 2, 23.
24. Mahlon Smith, "For Those Who Cast Stones," *The Fourth R* (May 1989), 2.
25. Graham Scott, interview with Michael McAteer.
26. John Dominic Crossan, interview with Michael McAteer.
27. Michael J. Wilkens and J. P. Moreland, eds., *Jesus Under Fire: Modern Scholarship Reinvents the Historical Jesus* (Grand Rapids, Mich.: Zondervan, 1994).
28. *The Mysteries of the Bible*, A&E television network (Arts and Entertainment).
29. John Dominic Crossan, interview with Michael McAteer.
30. John Dominic Crossan, *The Historical Jesus: The Life of a Mediterranean Peasant* (San Francisco: Harper, 1991), 425.
31. Robert Funk, in "Does the Bible give us Gospel truth on Jesus?" by Michael McAteer, *The Toronto Star* (Jan. 4, 1992), J9.

Chapter 2: Question and Answers

1. Cf. Bernard McGinn, *Antichrist: Two Thousand Years of Human Fascination with Evil* (San Francisco: Harper, 1994), 34.
2. Paula Fredriksen, *From Jesus to Christ: The Origins of the New Testament Images of Jesus* (New Haven/London: Yale University Press, 1988), xi.
3. Ethelbert Stauffer, *Jesus and His Story,* trans. Richard and Clara Winston (New York: Alfred A. Knopf, 1960), 59.

4. Uta Ranke-Heinemann, *Putting Away Childish Things: The Virgin Birth, the Empty Tomb and Other Fairy Tales You Don't Need to Believe to Have a Living Faith*, trans. Peter Heinegg (San Francisco: Harper, 1994), 2-3.
5. John Meier, *A Marginal Jew: Rethinking the Historical Jesus* (New York: Doubleday, 1991), 1:407.
6. S. Scott Barkley, professor of Christian Origins at UCLA, in the television series *Jesus and His Times*.
7. Ranke-Heinemann, *Putting Away Childish Things*, 3.
8. Stewart R. Sutherland, *God, Jesus and Belief: The Legacy of Theism* (Oxford: Basil Blackwell, 1984), 133.
9. Meier, *A Marginal Jew*, 1:5.
10. Albert Schweitzer, *The Quest of the Historical Jesus: A Critical Study of its Progress from Reimarus to Werde* (London: Adam & Charles Black, 1948), 396.
11. Bruce Barton, quoted in R. Laurence Moore, *Selling God: American Religion in the Marketplace of Culture* (New York/Oxford: Oxford University Press, 1994), 211.
12. Gerald Sheppard in "The Quest for Jesus" by Donna Sinclair, *The United Church Observer* (March 1995), 35.
13. Clifford Elliott, interview with Michael McAteer.
14. Jeffery Carlson, "Crossan's Jesus and Christian Identity," in *Jesus and Faith*, ed. Jeffrey Carlson and Robert A. Ludwig (Maryknoll, N.Y.: Orbis Books, 1994), 32.
15. John Meier, *A Marginal Jew*, 1:7.
16. Michael Green, "The Gospel Truth: Miracles Did Happen," *Christian Week* (Dec. 3, 1991), 1.
17. Edward Stillingford, in a letter to a Deist in 1677.
18. Craig Blomberg, "The Jesus Seminar: Searching for the 'Authentic Jesus,'" *Christian Research Journal* (Fall 1994), 35.
19. *The Toronto Star* (March 26, 1994), H19.
20. Flavius Josephus, *Jewish Antiquities*, 18:3.3.
21. Michael Arnheim, *Is Christianity True?* (Buffalo: Prometheus Books, 1984), 6.

22. Josephus, *Antiquities*, 20:9.1.

23. Arnheim, *Is Christianity True?*, 5.

24. Suetonius, *Claudius*, 25.

25. Tacitus, *Annals*, 15:44.2-8.

26. Joseph Klausner, *Jesus of Nazareth*, trans. Herbert Danby (New York: Macmillan, 1925), 18-24.

27. Bertrand Russell, *Why I Am Not a Christian* (London: George Allen & Unwin, 1957), 11-12.

28. R. Joseph Hoffman, *Jesus Outside the Gospels* (Buffalo: Prometheus Books, 1984), 127-128. Hoffmann is assistant professor of New Testament and Early Christian Studies at the University of Michigan.

29. McGinn, *Antichrist*, 34.

30. John Romer, *Testament: The Bible and History* (London: Michael O'Mara Books, 1988), 166.

31. Steve Humphries-Brooks is associate professor of Religion at Hamilton College, Clinton, New York. Interview with Michael McAteer.

32. John White, "Paul: A New Perspective," *The Fourth R* (Nov./Dec. 1993), 11.

33. Manfred Barthel, *What the Bible Really Says: Casting New Light on the Book of Books*, trans. and adapted by Mark Hawson (New York: William Morrow and Co., 1982), 291.

34. Dominic Crossan, interview with Michael McAteer.

35. Cf. Mathews, *The Clash of Gods*, 180.

Chapter 3: The Idols Fall

1. H. W. Janson, *History of Art* (New Jersey: Prentice Hall/New York: Harry N. Abrams, 1962), 149.

2. Cf. Karl Bihlmeyer and Herman Tüchle, *Church History*, vol. 1, *Christian Antiquity* (Westminster, Md.: The Newman Press, 1960), 98-99.

3. Robin Lane Fox, Pagans and Christians (New York: Knopf, 1987) 270.

4. Richard P. McBrien, *Catholicism: Completely Revised and Updated* (San Francisco: HarperCollins, 1994), 614-615.

5. Romer, *Testament*, 167.

6. Martin, *Oxford Illustrated History*, 70.

7. Romer, *Testament*, 167.

8. Koester, *Introduction to the New Testament*, 2:205-207.

9. Steve Mason, interview with Michael McAteer.

10. Cf. Elizabeth A. Livingston, *The Concise Oxford Dictionary of the Christian Church* (Oxford/London/New York: Oxford University Press, 1977), 561.

11. David Wenham, *Paul: Follower of Jesus or Founder of Christianity?* (Grand Rapids, Mich.: Eerdmans, 1995).

12. John Court, *The Church Times* (Sept. 15, 1995), 13.

13. Steve Mason, interview with Michael McAteer.

14. Richard Valantasis, interview with Michael Steinhauser.

15. Elaine Pagels, *The Origin of Satan* (New York: Random House, 1995), 66-67.

16. Charles W. Lowry, *The First Theologians* (Chicago: Gateway Editions, 1986) 95.

17. Geoffrey Barraclough, *The Christian World* (New York: Harry N. Abrams, 1981), 19.

18. Gal 2:4; cf. also Acts 20:30; Col. 2:18. *Concise Theological Dictionary*, 2e, ed. Karl Rahner and Herbert Vorgrimler (Tunbridge Wells, Kent: Burns and Oates, 1983), 46, 47.

19. Levy, *Blasphemy*, 36. The famous Christian philosopher Justin, along with six companions, was beheaded in A.D. 165.

20. Eusebius, *Ecc. Hist.*, 4, 17.

21. Peter De Rosa, *Vicars of Christ* (London: Corgi, 1989), 60.

22. Levy, *Blasphemy*, 41.

23. Ibid., 42.

24. Mathews, *The Clash of Gods*, 10.

25. Cf. Levy, *Blasphemy*, 43.
26. McBrien, *Catholicism*, 479.
27. Cf. Corinne Winter, *Encyclopedia of Catholicism* (San Francisco: HarperCollins, 1995), 529.
28. Ovey Mohammed is Professor of Systematic Theology at Toronto's Regis College. Cf. *Ecumenism* (December 1994) (Montreal: Canadian Centre for Ecumenism), 5.
29. John Dominic Crossan, interview with Michael McAteer.

Chapter 4: What is Truth?

1. From "The Everlasting Bible," *The Portable Bible* (New York: The Viking Press, 1968), quoted in Philip Yancey, *The Jesus I Never Knew* (Grand Rapids, Mich.: Zondervan, 1995), 612. Philip Yancey is editor-at-large for *The Christian Century*.
2. Romer, *Testament*, 332-333.
3. Carlson, "Crossan's Jesus," 32.
4. William Placher, "Is the Bible True?," *The Christian Century* (Oct. 11, 1995), 924.
5. Yancey, *The Jesus I Never Knew*, 13: 15-16. Interview with Michael McAteer.
6. *The Church of England Newspaper* (October 27, 1995), 4.
7. Wayne Meeks, ed., *The HarperCollins Study Bible* (New York: HarperCollins, 1993), 1857, 1915, 1953, 2011.
8. Mason, *Early Christian Reader*, x.
9. Kevin Orlin Johnson, *Why Do Catholics Do That?* (New York: Ballantine Books, 1994), 7.
10. Michael McAteer, "Biblical scholars spark reader response," *The Toronto Star* (June 17, 1988), M19.
11. Lowry, *The First Theologicans*, 17-18.
12. John Meier, introduction to *Introduction to the New Testament*, by Raymond Collins (New York: Image Books, 1987), xix.

13. Cf. Helmut Koester, *Ancient Christian Gospels: Their History and Development* (Philadelphia, Pa.: Trinity Press International, 1990) 35-36. Further in Helmut Koester, *Introduction to the New Testament*, 2 vols. (Berlin/New York: Walter de Gruyter, 1982), 2:8-9.

14. Irenaeus, *Against Heresies*, 1,3:11.9.

15. Pagels, *The Origin of Satan*, 69.

16. Ibid., 70.

17. Eusebius, *Ecc. Hist.*, 3:25.4.

18. Roy Hoover, "How the Canon was Determined," *The Fourth R*, vol. 5, no. 1 (1992), 1-7.

19. Collins, *Introduction*, 88.

20. Romer, *Testament*, 234.

21. Cf. Collins, *Introduction*, 36-37.

22. David C. Fowler, *The Bible in Early English Literature* (Washington: University of Washington Press, 1976), 148.

23. Gerald Bray, ed., *Documents of the English Reformation* (Minneapolis: Fortress Press, 1994), 17.

24. Fowler, *The Bible in Early English Literature*, 149.

25. Romer, *Testament*, 307.

26. Hans Rudi Weber, *The Book that Reads Me* (Geneva: World Council of Churches Publication, 1995), 16.

27. Bruce M. Metzger and Michael D. Coogan, eds., *The Oxford Companion to the Bible* (New York: Oxford University Press, 1993), 759.

28. Hoover, "How the Canon was Determined," 7.

29. Collins, *Introduction*, 2.

30. Neil Asher Silberman, "Searching for Jesus," *Archaeology* (Nov./Dec. 1994), 32.

31. James Charlesworth, *Jesus and the Dead Sea Scrolls* (New York: Doubleday, 1992), 40.

32. Collins, *Introduction*, 4.

33. Pagels, *The Origin of Satan*, 65-66.

34. Pope John Paul II, *Crossing the Threshold of Hope* (Toronto: Alfred A. Knopf, 1994), 90.

35. Pagels, *The Gnostic Gospels*, 151.

36. Helmut Koester, *Ancient Christian Gospels: Their History and Development* (London: SCM Press, 1990), 85-86.

37. Robert J. Miller, ed., *The Complete Gospels: Annotated Scholars Version* (Sonoma, Calif.: Polebridge Press, 1992), 3-4.

38. Gospel of Mary, 10:3, in Miller, *The Complete Gospels*, 359.

39. Pagels, *The Gnostic Gospels*, 64-65.

40. The Infancy Gospel of Thomas, 4:1-2, in Miller, *The Complete Gospels*, 366.

41. Infancy Gospel of Thomas, 6, in Miller, *The Complete Gospels*, 367.

42. Miller, *The Complete Gospels*, 3.

43. Johnson, *Why Do Catholics Do That?*, 21.

44. David Bartlett, "The Historical Life of Jesus and the Life of Faith," *The Christian Century* (May 6, 1992), 490

Chapter 5: Dissenting Voices

1. Kenneth Clarke, *Civilization: A Personal View* (New York: Doubleday, 1995), 44.

2. Karen Armstrong, *History of God: The 4000-Year Quest of Judaism, Christianity and Islam* (New York: Alfred A. Knopf, 1993), 289.

3. Cf. Stuart Kaufman, *At Home in the Universe* (New York: Oxford University Press, 1995), 6.

4. Weber, *The Book that Reads Me*, 13.

5. Cf. Clark, *Civilization*, 262.

6. Clarke, *Civilization*, 159.

7. Armstrong, *History of God*, 275.

8. E. Royston Pike, *Slayers of Superstition* (Port Washington, N.Y.: Kennibat Press, 1970), 25.

9. John McManners, ed., *The Oxford Illustrated History of Christianity* (Oxford: Oxford University Press, 1990), 282.

10. Mason, *An Early Christian Reader*, 101.

11. Jaroslav Pelikan, *Jesus through the Centuries* (New York: Yale University Press, 1985), 187.

12. Cf. James M. Robinson, *A New Quest of the Historical Jesus*, Studies in Biblical Theology (London: SCM Press, 1959), 27-28.

13. For an excellent introduction to Reimarus and his writings see Charles H. Talbert, ed., *Reimarus: Fragments*, trans. Ralph S. Fraser, *Lives of Jesus Series*, ed. Leander E. Keck (Philadelphia: Fortress Press, 1970).

14. Marcus Borg, "Reimarus and the Beginning of the Quest," *The Fourth R* (Nov. 1991), 8.

15. Albert Schweitzer, *The Quest of the Historical Jesus : A Critical Study of its Progress from Reimarus to Werde* (London: Adam & Clarles Black, 1948), 13-14.

16. For English influence on Reimarus see Talbert, *Reimarus: Fragments*, 14-18.

17. Elizabeth Livingstone, *The Concise Oxford Dictionary of the Christian Church* (Oxford: Oxford University Press, 1977), 433.

18. Ibid., 490.

19. Donald F. Winslow, *Anglican Theological Review* (Cambridge, Mass.: Episcopal Divinity School, Spring 1992), 228.

20. W. Barnes Tatum, *In Quest of Jesus: A Guide Book* (Louisville: John Knox Press, 1982), 162.

21. John S. Kselman, "Modern New Testament Criticism," *The Jerome Biblical Commentary*, ed. Raymond E. Brown, Joseph A. Fitzmyer, and Roland Murphy (New Jersey: Prentice Hall, 1968), 2:9.

22. Gerd Lüdemann, *The Resurrection of Jesus: History, Experience, Theology*, trans. John Bowden (London: SCM Press, 1994), 181.

23. N. T. Wright, "The Historical Jesus," *Anchor Dictionary of the Bible* (New York: Doubleday, 1992), 2:797.

24. Neil Asher Silberman, "Searching for Jesus," *Archaeology* (Nov./Dec. 1994), 31. Neil Asher Silberman is a contributing editor to *Archaeology* and author of *The Hidden Scrolls* and *The War for the Dead Sea Scrolls*.

25. Kselman, "Modern New Testament Criticism," 2:13.
26. William Wrede, *The Messianic Secret*, trans. J. C. D. Greig (Greenwood, S.C.: Attic Press, 1971).
27. Kselman, "Modern New Testament Criticism," 2:12.
28. Collins, *Introduction*, 400.
29. Schweitzer, *Quest*, 396-7.
30. Günther Bornkamm, *Jesus of Nazareth*, trans. Irene and Fraser McLuskey with James M. Robinson (New York/Evanston/London: Harper & Row, 1960), 12-13.
31. Wright, "Quest for the Historical Jesus," 3:798.

Chapter 6: "The More, the Merrier"

1. Cf. *Christian Century* (August 24-31, 1994), 784-787.
2. W. Barnes Tatum, *In Quest of Jesus: A Guidebook* (Louisville: John Knox Press), 71.
3. Schweitzer, *Quest*, 399; cf. Tatum, *In Quest of Jesus*, 71.
4. Cf. Tatum, *In Quest of Jesus*, 72.
5. Arnheim, *Is Christianity True?*, 4.
6. Rudolf Bultmann, *The History of the Synoptic Tradition*, trans. John Marsh (Oxford: Basil Blackwell, 1963), 370.
7. Arnheim, *Is Christianity True?*, 4.
8. James N. Robinson, interview with Michael Steinhauser.
9. Ernst Käsemann, "The Problem of the Historical Jesus," *Essays on New Testament Themes*, trans. by W. J. Montague, Studies in Biblical Theology (London: SCM Press, 1964), 45.
10. Cf. Ernst Käsemann, "Problem of the Historical Jesus," 45-46.
11. Cf. Luke 11:2; Mark 14:36.; cf. Norman Perrin and Dennis C. Duling, *The New Testament: An Introduction* (New York: Harcourt Brace Jovanovich, 1972), 405.
12. Cf. Luke 11:2; Mark 14:36.; Matt. 6:9; Gal. 4:6; Rom. 8:15; cf. Perrin and Duling, *The New Testament*, 405.

13. Rudolf Bultmann, *History of the Synoptic Tradition*, 219.
14. Cf. Günther Bornkamm, *Jesus of Nazareth*, 172.
15. Tatum, *In Quest of Jesus*, 76.
16. Cf. S. G. F. Brandon, *Jesus and the Zealots: A Study of the Political Factors in Primitive Christianity* (New York: Charles Scribner' Sons 1967); Morton Smith, *Jesus the Magician* (New York: Harper & Row, 1978); Morton Smith, *The Secret Gospel of Mark* (Cambridge, Mass.: Harvard University Press, 1973).
17. James M. Robinson, interview with Michael Steinhauser.
18. Cf. Marcus J. Borg, "New Energy in Quest for the Historical Jesus," *Compass* (January/February 1993), 10-11. Also see Marcus J. Borg, "Portraits of Jesus in Contemporary North American Scholarship," *Harvard Theological Review*, 84:1 (1991), 1-22.
19. Wright, "Quest for the Historical Jesus," 800.
20. Eric M. Meyer and James F. Strange, *Archaeology, the Rabbis, and Early Christianity: The Social and Historical Setting of Palestinian Judaism and Christianity* (Nashville: Abingdon Press, 1981).
21. Richard A. Horsley, *Sociology and the Jesus Movement* (New York: Crossroad, 1989), 78.
22. N. Thomas Wright, interview with Michael Steinhauser.
23. Geza Vermes, *Jesus the Jew: A Historian's Reading of the Gospels* (London: SCM Press, 1973), 223.
24. Bruce Chilton, interview with Michael Steinhauser.
25. E. P. Sanders, *Jesus and Judaism* (Philadelphia: Fortress Press, 1985). 319.
26. Burton L. Mack, *The Myth of Innocence: Mark and Christian Origins* (Philadelphia: Fortress Press, 1988), 67-69.
27. Leif E. Vaage, *Galilean Upstarts: Jesus' First Followers According to Q* (Valley Forge, Pa.: Trinity Press International, 1995), 88.
28. James M. Robinson, interview with Michael Steinhauser.
29. Marcus J. Borg, *Conflict, Holiness and Politics in the Teaching of Jesus* (1984) and *Jesus, A New Vision: Spirit, Culture, and the Life of Discipleship* (San Francisco: Harper, 1991).

30. Daniel Fraikin, interview with Michael Steinhauser.

31. Steve Humphries-Brooks, interview with Michael McAteer.

32. Cf. Thomas Aquinas Collins and Raymond E. Brown, "Church Pronouncements," *Jerome Biblical Commentary*, 2:72:6.

33. John Dominic Crossan, *The Historical Jesus: The Life of a Mediterranean Jewish Peasant* (San Francisco, Calif.: Harper, 1991.), xxx.

34. Ibid., 19.

35. Ibid., 298.

36. John P. Meier, *A Marginal Jew*, 1:41, 117, 139.

37. John P. Meier, "Jesus," *New Jerome Biblical Commentary* (Englewood Cliffs, N.J.: Prentice Hall, 1990), 1317.

38. Daniel Fraikin, interview with Michael Steinhauser.

39. Helmut Koester, *Ancient Christian Gospels*, 86.

40. 1 Cor. 15:3ff. Cf. William Farmer, *The Gospel Of Jesus: The Pastoral Relevance of the Synoptic Problem* (Louisville, Ky.: Westminster/John Knox Press, 1994), 178.

41. Farmer, *The Gospel of Jesus*, 3.

Chapter 7: The Empty Tomb

1. Wilton Barnhardt, *Gospel* (New York: St. Martin's Press, 1993), 210.

2. Klausner, *Jesus of Nazareth*, 356.

3. Ben Meyer, interview with Michael McAteer.

4. Michael Arnheim, *Is Christianty True?* (Buffalo: Prometheus Books, 1984), 6, 7, 146.

5. Elaine Pagels, *The Gnostic Gospels*, 3-6.

6. Marianne Sawicki, "Easter Narrative: What Really Happened?", *National Catholic Reporter* (April 14, 1995), 10.

7. Bart Ehrman, "Mysteries of the Bible," Arts and Entertainment Television.

8. John L. Collins, *The Sceptre and the Star* (New York: Doubleday Dell, 1995), 209-210.

9. Robert Funk, "How Jesus Became God," *The Fourth R* (Nov. 1991), 4.

10. Johannes Quasten, *Patrology* (Utrecht-Antwwerp: Spectrum Publishers, 1975), 1:196.

11. J. N. D. Kelly, *Early Christian Doctrines*, 141.

12. Ignatius, *Trall.*, 10; *Smyrn.*, 2.

13. Cf. Kelly, *Early Christian Doctrines*, 139-141; Jean Daniélou, *The Theology of Jewish Christianity* (London: Darton, Longman & Todd, 1964), 56.

14. William Lane Craig, *Jesus Under Fire*, eds. Michael F. Wilkins and J. P. Moreland (Grand Rapids: Zondervan Publishing, 1994), 165.

15. A. N. Wilson, *C. S. Lewis: A Biography* (Glasgow: Collins, 1990), 163.

16. Ibid., 164-165.

17. Jackson Carrol, in Nancy Gibbs, "The Message of Miracles," *Time* (April 10, 1995), 43.

18. David Bartlett, "The Historical Jesus and the Life of Faith," *The Christian Century* (May 6, 1995), 491.

19. John A. T. Robinson, *Honest to God* (London: SCM Press, 1971), 70.

20. Hans Conzelmann, *An Outline of the Theology of the New Testament* (London: SCM Press, 1969), 77.

21. Joseph A. Fitzmyer, S.J., *Paul and His Theology: A Brief Sketch* (Engelwood, N.J.: Prentice Hall, 1989), 50.

22. John 1:1. Cf. Raymond E. Brown, S.S., *The Birth of the Messiah: A Commentary on the Infancy Narratives in Matthew and Luke* (New York: Doubleday, 1977), 29-32.

23. Raymond E. Brown, *The Gospel According to John*, 2 vols. (New York: Doubleday, 1966), 1:524.

24. Larry Hurtado, interview with Michael Steinhauser.

25. Royston E. Pike, *Slayers of Superstition*, 50.

26. David Jenkins in "The 'outspoken' bishop is coming to town," by Michael McAteer, *The Toronto Star* (Sept. 16, 1989), M19.
27. John Spong, interview with Michael McAteer.
28. Jesus Seminar press release, 6 March, 1995.
29. Kevin Quast, interview with Michael McAteer.
30. Michael McAteer, "Scholars paint radical picture of 'real' Jesus," *The Toronto Star* (April 10, 1993), A2.
31. Craig, *Jesus Under Fire*, 142
32. James Dickey, interview with Michael McAteer.
33. Larry Hurtado, interview with Michael Steinhauser.

Chapter 8: What's Left for Sunday?

1. Chris Shea, interview with Michael Steinhauser. Elmer Gantry is a figure in Sinclair Lewis's novel of the same name, a hypocritical pastor who has one moving sermon that he uses on numerous occasions.
2. Andrew Greeley, "Historical Jesus Remains Elusive to All Search Parties," *Arizona Republic* (Jan. 21, 1995).
3. John Robinson, *Honest to God* (London: SCM Press, 1963), 30-34, 130-135.
4. Don Carson, professor of New Testament, Trinity Evangelical Divinity School, in the television documentary "The Life and Times of Jesus."
5. Josephus, *Against Apion*, 2:42.293.
6. Robert Bater, interview with Michael Steinhauser.
7. Gordon Melton, introduction to *Religious Tolerance and Religious Diversity* (Santa Barbara: The Institute for the Study of American Religion, 1995), 2.
8. Michael McAteer, "United Church faces new fears," *The Toronto Star* (June 29, 1991), G9.
9. Don Posterski, interview with Michael McAteer.

10. Larry Hurtado, interview with Michael Steinhauser.

11. Raymond Humphries, interview with Michael Steinhauser.

12. Ben Meyer, interview with Michael McAteer. Hermeneutics is the theory of interpretation, particularly of biblical texts.

13. Terry Prendergast, interview with Michael McAteer.

14. Douglas Hall, interview with Michael McAteer.

15. Russell Shorto, *GQ* (June 1994), 175.

16. Ecumenical News Service, Geneva, September 1995.

17. Graham Scott, interview with Michael McAteer.

18. N. Thomas Wright, interview with Michael Steinhauser.

19. Gustav Niebuhr, "Who Was Jesus? A Search for Clues Grows," *The New York Times* (December 25, 1994), 1.

20. Neil Asher Silberman, "Searching for Jesus," *Archaeology* (Nov./Dec. 1994), 31.

21. Cf. Philip Hill, New York Times Service in *The Globe and Mail* (April 3, 1995), A9.

22. Don Cupitt, *After All: Religion Without Alienation* (London: SCM, 1994),.

23. Don Cupitt, "Don Cupitt's Gospel," *John Cornwell Tablet Magazine* (Aug. 6, 1994), 979-980.

24. Steve Humphries-Brooks, interview with Michael McAteer.

25. Marcus Borg, *The Fourth R*, vol. 7, no. 5 (Sept./Oct.1995), 4.

26. Leander Keck, "The Second Coming of the Liberal Jesus?", *The Christian Century* (Aug. 24-31, 1994), 787.

27. Ecumenical News International Bulletin (Nov. 1995)

28. *Church Times* (July 28, 1995), 13.

29. Kenton Robinson, "Error in Christ's Birthdate Could Mean Millenium Already Here," *The Hartford Courant* (Jan. 19, 1995).

30. John Dominic Crossan, "The Life of a Mediterranean Peasant," *The Christian Century* (Dec. 18-25, 1991), 1203.

31. Sutherland, *God, Jesus and Belief*, 142-143.

Timeline

27 B.C.–A.D. **14** Reign of Augustus Caesar, who united the known world under Roman Law and ushered in a period of peace. During his reign, Jesus was born. The exact year of Jesus' birth remains a moot point. Most evidence points to his birth between 2 and 6 B.C. Many scholars accept 4 B.C. as the date. For the purposes of this timeline, the commonly accepted date of 1 A.D. has been used.

27 Baptism of Jesus by John the Baptist, a prophetic figure who preached the imminent coming of God's judgement. Jesus begins his ministry after John is put to death on the orders of King Herod, ca. 28/29

33 After a short ministry centred in Galilee, Jesus is crucified. Reports that he rose from the dead circulate among his scattered followers who regroup and begin the dissemination of his message.

34 After a dramatic experience on the road to Damascus, Paul, a zealous anti-Christian Jew from Tarsus, accepts Jesus as Lord and becomes one the most influential figures in Christian history. Until his execution in Rome in 64, Paul is instrumental in spreading Christianity to Gentiles outside Palestine. His letters to young Christian communities are part of the New Testament.

66–100 The four Gospels of Matthew, Mark, Luke, and John are written by unknown authors. Mark is believed to have been the earliest of the four Gospels, and John, the latest. Acts of the Apostles, a companion volume to the Gospel of Luke, is believed to have been written between 85-90.

144 Marcion, a bishop's son from Sinope on the Black Sea preaches a Christianity that denies all Jewish connections with Jesus. He proposes that the church reject the Jewish Scriptures and embrace a new canon—a non-Jewish Bible with one Gospel, Luke, and one Apostle, Paul. Marcion is later excommunicated.

182-188 Iraeneus, Bishop of Lyon, writes his monumental work *Against Heresies*. He refutes and condemns many early heresies, including that of Marcion. In this work he argues for the inclusion of the Gospels of Matthew, Mark, Luke, and John into the canon.

312 Prompted by a heavenly command, Constantine adopts a Christian symbol for his standard and defeats his rival Maxentius. Constantine becomes western emperor of Roman Empire.

313 Constantine and Licinius, emperor of the eastern Roman Empire, issue the Edict of Milan, which tolerates all cults including Christianity. This allows Christianity to surface.

324 Constantine defeats Licinius and becomes sole ruler of the Roman Empire. He sets about uniting a divided Christianity rife with heresies by convening the Council of Nicaea in 325. Council condemns Arian preaching and produces what later becomes known as the Nicene Creed, which affirms that the Son is equal in status to the Father. Subsequent councils over the centuries (Ephesus, Chalcedon, Constantine among them) attempt to resolve theological disputes about the nature of Christ and the Trinity.

325 Eusebius, bishop, historian, and Constantine's secretary, names twenty-one books that should be included in what was to become known as the New Testament.

367 Athanasius, Bishop of Alexandria, issues the first list that tallies with the contents of our current New Testament.

384 Jerome, directed by Pope Damascus, produces the Vulgate or Common Bible, the first revised text of the four Latin Gospels.

1380 John Wycliffe produces the first English version of the Bible, which is condemned as heretical.

ca. **1450** Johann Gutenburg prints the Latin Bible on his invention, the printing press.

1517 Luther issues his list of ninety-five criticisms of church practices and launches the Protestant Reformation. He later translates the Bible into German for a Reformed Church. He is excommunicated in 1521.

1526 William Tyndale's English translation of the New Testament is printed in Worms, Germany. It was to be the bedrock upon which the 1611 Authorized King James Version of the Bible was set.

1546 Council of Trent declares writings of Jerome's Latin Vulgate version to be the Roman Catholic Church's official canon.

The Quest

Old Quest

1774-78 Gotthold Lessing publishes fragments of the work of German scholar Samuel Reimarus who died in 1768. Called the father of historical Jesus scholarship, Reimarus portrays Jesus as failed messianic pretender and argues that the words of the Gospels are falsifications.

1835 David Frederick Strauss publishes *The Life of Christ Critically Examined*. He argues that it is impossible to write a life of Jesus because what we know about him come from the evangelists, who were expressing their own faith in Jesus.

1859 English naturalist Charles Darwin publishes *The Origin of Species*, suggesting that higher forms of life descend from lower forms.

1863 H. J. Holzman publishes his monumental *The Synoptic Gospels: Their Origin and Historical Character*, postulating the "two source" theory that Mark's Gospel and a hypothetical sayings source known as "Q" were used by Matthew and Luke.

1863 Publication of Ernest Renan's *Life of Jesus* causes a sensation by stripping Christianity of its supernatural trappings and presenting Jesus as just a man.

1901 William Wrede's book *The Messianic Secret* argues that the dilemma of historical Jesus research lies in the very nature of the sources themselves. He argues that Jesus' messiahship is the creation of a post-resurrection Christian community.

1906 Albert Schweitzer's *The Quest for the Historical Jesus* reviews the major works on the historical Jesus and concludes that further attempts to writes books on the life of the historical Jesus would be futile.

No Quest

The period from the publication of Schweitzer's *The Quest for the Historical Jesus* to the early 1950s is known as the "no quest" period because it was dominated by the scepticism of Rudolf Bultmann, one of this century's most prominent theologians. Bultmann contended that since the Gospels and the traditions incorporated in them were written after Jesus' resurrection, it was impossible, even illegitimate, to use them for information about the historical Jesus.

New Quest

1953 German professor Ernst Käsemann lectures to a gathering of Bultmann's former students,' arguing that there is some central point around which something like a life of Jesus could be constructed.

1956 Günther Bornkamm's book *Jesus of Nazareth* popularizes Käsemann's lecture. Bornkamm regards the miracles narrated in the Gospels, not as remarkable historical occurrences, but as events seen through the eyes of the early church.

Third Quest

1973-1978 Meeting of Society of Biblical Literature Seminar on the Parables awakens interest in North America in the historical Jesus.

1985-1989 Society of Biblical Literature seminar on "Q" led by James M. Robinson contributes a whole new picture of Jesus as a wisdom teacher.

1985 Robert Funk launches the Jesus Seminar to enquire into the sayings and deeds of Jesus. Publications: *The Parables of Jesus: Red Letter Edition* (1988); *The Gospel of Mark: Red Letter Edition* (1991); *The Complete Gospels* (1992); *The Five Gospels* (1993).

1991 Dominic Crossan publishes *The Historical Jesus*.

1991 John Meier publishes the first volume of *A Marginal Jew*. The second volume is published in 1994.

1994 Marcus Borg publishes *Meeting Jesus Again for the First Time*.

Bibliography

The following is a list of books used by the authors in their research. References to interviews and to articles in *The Fourth R*, a Westar Institute publication that reports on the Jesus Seminar, have been omitted here. Such references and other sources are found in the notes.

Armstrong, Karen. *A History of God: The 4000-Year Quest of Judaism, Christianity and Islam*. New York: Alfred A. Knopf, 1993.

Arnheim, Michael. *Is Christianity True?* Buffalo: Prometheus Books, 1984.

Baigent, Michael; Richar Leigh and Henry Lincoln. *The Messianic Legacy*. New York: A Gorgi Book, 1988.

Barraclough, Geoffrey. *The Christian World*. New York: Harry N. Abrams, 1981.

Barthel, Manfred. *What the Bible Really Says: Casting New Light on the Book of Books*. Translated and adapted by Mark Hawson. New York: William Morrow and Co., 1982.

Bartlett, David. "The Historical Jesus and the Life of Faith." *The Christian Century* (May 6, 1992): 491.

Borg, Marcus J. *Conflict, Holiness and Politics in the Teachings of Jesus*. Studies in the Bible and Early Christianity, vol. 5. New York/Toronto: Edwin Mellen Press, 1984.

_____. "A Temperate Case for a Non-eschatological Jesus." *Forum* 2/3 (1986): 81-102.

_____. *Jesus A New Vision: Spirit, Culture, and the Life of Discipleship.* San Francisco: Harper, 1991.

_____. *Jesus in Contemporary Scholarship.* Valley Forge, Pa.: Trinity Press International, 1994.

_____. *Meeting Jesus Again for the First Time: The Historical Jesus and the Heart of Contemporary Faith.* San Francisco: Harper, 1994.

Bornkamm, Günther. *Jesus of Nazareth.* Translated by Irene and Fraser McLuskey with James M. Robinson. New York/Evanston/London: Harper & Row, 1960.

Brandon, S. G. F. *Jesus and the Zealots: A Study of the Political Factors in Primitive Christianity.* Manchester: Manchester University Press, 1967.

Bray, Gerald, ed. *Documents of the English Reformation.* Minneapolis: Fortress Press, 1994.

Brown, Raymond E. *The Birth of the Messiah: A Commentary on the Infancy Narratives in Matthew and Luke.* New York: Doubleday, 1977.

Bultmann, Rudolf. *The History of the Synoptic Tradition.* Translated by John Marsh. Oxford: Basil Blackwell, 1963.

Cahill, Thomas. *How the Irish Saved Civilization: The Untold Story of Ireland's Heroic Role from the Fall of Rome to the Rise of Medieval Europe.* New York: Doubleday, 1995.

Carlson, Jeffrey and Robert A. Ludwig. *Jesus and Faith: A Conversation on the Work of John Dominic Crossan*. MaryKnoll, N.Y.: Orbis Books, 1993.

Carmichael, Joel. *The Death of Jesus*. New York: Macmillan, 1962.

Catechism of the Catholic Church. New York/London/Toronto: Doubleday, 1994.

Cassels, Louis. *This Fellow Jesus*. Anderson, Indiana: Warner Press, 1973.

Chadwick, Henry, and G. R. Evans, eds. *Atlas of the Christian Church*. New York: Equinox Book, 1987.

Charlesworth, James. *Jesus and the Dead Sea Scrolls*. New York: Doubleday, 1992.

Chilton, Bruce D. *A Galilean Rabbi and His Bible: Jesus' Use of the Interpreted Scripture of His Time*. Wilmington, Del.: Glazier, 1984.

Clark, Kenneth. *Civilization: A Personal View*. New York/Evanston: Harper & Row, 1969.

Collins, John J. *The Scepter and the Star: The Messiahs of the Dead Sea Scrolls and Other Ancient Literature*. The Anchor Bible Reference Library. Edited by David Noel Freedman. New York: Doubleday, 1995.

Collins, Raymond. *Introduction to the New Testament*. New York: Doubleday, Image Book, 1987.

Conzelmann, Hans. *An Outline of the Theology of the New Testament*. London: SCM Press, 1969.

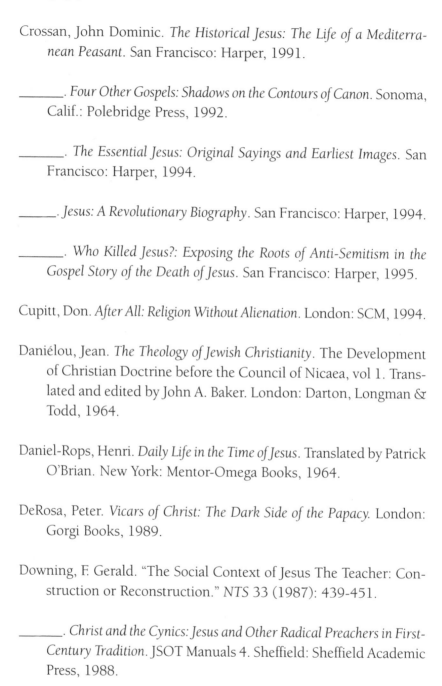

Crossan, John Dominic. *The Historical Jesus: The Life of a Mediterranean Peasant*. San Francisco: Harper, 1991.

_____. *Four Other Gospels: Shadows on the Contours of Canon*. Sonoma, Calif.: Polebridge Press, 1992.

_____. *The Essential Jesus: Original Sayings and Earliest Images*. San Francisco: Harper, 1994.

_____. *Jesus: A Revolutionary Biography*. San Francisco: Harper, 1994.

_____. *Who Killed Jesus?: Exposing the Roots of Anti-Semitism in the Gospel Story of the Death of Jesus*. San Francisco: Harper, 1995.

Cupitt, Don. *After All: Religion Without Alienation*. London: SCM, 1994.

Daniélou, Jean. *The Theology of Jewish Christianity*. The Development of Christian Doctrine before the Council of Nicaea, vol 1. Translated and edited by John A. Baker. London: Darton, Longman & Todd, 1964.

Daniel-Rops, Henri. *Daily Life in the Time of Jesus*. Translated by Patrick O'Brian. New York: Mentor-Omega Books, 1964.

DeRosa, Peter. *Vicars of Christ: The Dark Side of the Papacy*. London: Gorgi Books, 1989.

Downing, F. Gerald. "The Social Context of Jesus The Teacher: Construction or Reconstruction." *NTS* 33 (1987): 439-451.

_____. *Christ and the Cynics: Jesus and Other Radical Preachers in First-Century Tradition*. JSOT Manuals 4. Sheffield: Sheffield Academic Press, 1988.

Encyclopedic Dictionary of Religion. Washington, D.C.: Corpus, 1979.

Falk, Harvey. *Jesus the Pharisee: A New Look at the Jewishness of Jesus.* New York/Mahwah: Paulist Press, 1985.

Farmer, William, R. *The Gospel of Jesus: The Pastoral Relevance of the Synoptic Problem.* Louisville, Ky.: Westminster/John Knox, 1994.

Fitzmyer, Joseph A. S.J. *Paul and His Theology: A Brief Sketch.* New Jersey: Prentice Hall, 1989.

The Five Gospels: The Search for the Authentic Words of Jesus. New translation and commentary by Robert W. Funk, Roy H. Hoover, and the Jesus Seminar. New York: Macmillan, 1993.

Fredriksen, Paula. *From Jesus to Christ: The Origins of the New Testament Images of Jesus.* New Haven/London: Yale University Press, 1988.

Fuller, Reginald H. *The Foundations of New Testament Christology.* London: Lutterworth, 1965.

Funk, Robert W., Bernard Brandon Scott, and James R. Butts. *The Parables of Jesus: Red Letter Edition; A Report of the Jesus Seminar.* Sonoma, Calif.: Polebridge Press, 1988.

Funk, Robert W., and Mahlon H. Smith. *The Gospel of Mark: Red Letter Edition.* Sonoma, Calif.: Polebridge Press, 1990.

Funk, Robert W., Roy W. Hoover, and the Jesus Seminar. *The Five Gospels: The Search for the Authentic Words of Jesus.* New York: Macmillan, 1993.

Gardner, Martin. *The Way of a Philosophical Scrivener*. New York: Quill, 1983.

Hall, Douglas John. *The Future of the Church*. Toronto: The United Church Publishing House, 1989.

The HarperCollins Study Bible: Revised Standard Version with Apocryphal/Deuterocanonical Books. General editor, Wayne Meeks. London: HarperCollins, 1993.

Hengel, Martin. *The Son of God: The Origin of Christology and History of Jewish-Hellenistic Religion*. Philadelphia: Fortress Press, 1976.

Hoffmann, R. Joseph. *Jesus Outside the Gospels*. Buffalo: Prometheus Books, 1984.

Horsely, Richard A. *Jesus and the Spiral of Violence: Popular Jewish Resistance in Roman Palestine*. San Francisco: Harper & Row, 1987.

_____. *Sociology and the Jesus Movement*. New York: Crossroads, 1989.

Hurtado, Larry W. *One God, One Lord: Early Christian Devotion and Ancient Jewish Monotheism*. Philadelphia: Fortress Press, 1988.

Johnson, Kevin Orlin. *Why Do Catholics Do That?* New York: Ballantine Books, 1994.

Käsemann, Ernst. "The Problem of the Historical Jesus." *Essays on New Testament Themes*. Translated by W. J. Montague. Studies in Biblical Theology. London: SCM Press, 1964.

Kauffman, Stuart. *At Home in the Universe*. New York: Oxford University Press, 1995.

Kelly, J. N. D. *Early Christian Doctrines*. New York/Evanston/London: Harper & Row, 1960.

Kselman, John S. "Modern New Testament Criticism." *The Jerome Biblical Commentary*. Edited by Raymond E. Brown, Joseph A. Fitzmyer, and Roland Murphy. New Jersey: Prentice Hall, 1968.

Klausner, Joseph. *Jesus of Nazareth*. Translated by Herbert Danby. New York: Macmillan, 1925.

Kloppenborg, John S. *The Formation of Q: Trajectories in Ancient Wisdom Collections*. Studies in Antiquity and Christianity. Philadelphia: Fortress Press, 1987.

Kloppenborg, John S., Marvin W. Meyer, Stephen J. Patterson, and Michael G. Steinhauser. *Q—Thomas Reader*. Sonoma, Calif.: Polebridge Press, 1990.

Koester, Helmut. *Introduction to the New Testament*. 2 vols. Berlin/New York: Walter de Gruyter, 1982.

_____. *Ancient Christian Gospels: Their History and Development*. Philadelphia Pa.: Trinity International Press; London: SCM Press, 1990.

Lane Fox, Robin. *Pagans and Christians*. New York: Alfred A. Knopf, 1987.

Laurence, Moore R. *Selling God: American Religion in the Marketplace of Culture*. New York/Oxford: Oxford University Press, 1994.

Lerner, Gerda. *Creation of Feminist Consciousness*. New York: Oxford University Press, 1993.

Levy, Leonard W. *Blasphemy: Verbal Offense against the Sacred from Moses to Salman Rushdie*. New York: Alfred A. Knopf, 1993.

Lewis, C. S. *Fern-Seed and Elephants and other Essays on Christianity*. Edited by Walter Hooper. Glasgow: Collins/Fountain Books, 1975.

Livingstone, Elizabeth A. *The Concise Oxford Dictionary of the Christian Church*. Oxford/London/New York: Oxford University Press, 1977.

Lowry, Charles W. *The First Theologicans*. Chicago: Gateway Editions, 1986.

Lüdemann, Gerd. *The Resurrection of Jesus: History, Experience, Theology*. Translated by John Bowden. London: SCM Press, 1994.

Mack, Burton L. *The Myth of Innocence: Mark and Christian Origins*. Philadelphia: Fortress Press, 1987.

Mason, Steve, and Tom Robinson. *An Early Christian Reader*. Toronto: Canadian Scholars Press, 1990.

_____. *Josephus and the New Testament*. Peabody, Mass.: Hendrickson, 1992.

Mathews, Thomas F. *The Clash of Gods: A Reinterpretation of Early Christian Art*. Princeton, Pa.: Princeton University Press, 1993.

McBrien, Richard P. *Catholicism: Completely Revised and Updated*. San Francisco: HarperCollins, 1994.

_____., ed. *The HarperCollins Encyclopedia of Catholicism*. San Francisco: Harper, 1995.

McGinn, Bernard. *Antichrist: Two Thousand Years of Human Fascination with Evil*. San Francisco: Harper, 1994.

Meier, John P. *A Marginal Jew: Rethinking the Historical Jesus*. 2 vols. New York: Doubleday, 1991-1994.

Meyer, Eric M., and James F. Strange. *Archaeology, the Rabbis, and Early Christianity: The Social and Historical Setting of Palestinian Judaism and Christianity*. Nashville: Abingdon Press, 1981.

Miller, Robert J., ed. *The Complete Gospels: Annotated Scholars Version*. Sonoma, Calif.: Polebridge Press, 1992.

Moore, R. Laurence. *Selling God: American Religion in the Marketplace of Culture*. New York/Oxford: Oxford University Press, 1994.

The Nag Hammadi Library in English. Translated by Members of the Coptic Library Project of the Institute for Antiquity and Christianity. James M. Robinson, Director. San Francisco: Harper & Row, 1977.

Pagels, Elaine. *The Gnostic Gospels*. New York: Randon House, 1979.

_____. *The Origin of Satan*. New York: Random House, 1995.

Perrin, Norman, and Dennis C. Duling. *The New Testament: An Introduction. Proclamation and Parenesis, Myth and History*. New York: Harcourt Brace Jovanovich, 1974.

Pike, E. Royston. *Slayers of Superstition*. Port Washington, N.Y.: Kennikat Press, 1970.

The Portable Bible. New York: The Viking Press, 1968.

Posterski, Donald C. *True to You: Living our Faith in our Multi-minded World*. Winfield, B.C.: Woodlake Books, 1995.

Rahner, Karl, and Herbert Vorgrimler, eds. *Concise Theological Dictionary*. Second edition. Tunbridge Wells, Kent: Burns and Oates, 1983.

Ranke-Heinemann, Uta. *Putting Away Childish Things: The Virgin Birth, the Empty Tomb and Other Fairy Tales You Don't Need to Believe to Have a Living Faith*. Translated by Peter Heinegg. San Francisco: Harper, 1994.

Robinson, James M. *A New Quest of the Historical Jesus*. Studies in Biblical Theology. London: SCM Press, 1963.

Robinson, John A. T. *Honest to God*. London: SCM Press, 1963.

Romer, John. *Testament: The Bible and History*. London: Michael O'Mara Books, 1988.

Sanders, E. P. *Jesus and Judaism*. Philadelphia: Fortress Press, 1985.

_____. *The Historical Figure of Jesus*. London: Penguin Press, 1993.

Schweitzer, Albert. *The Quest of the Historical Jesus: A Critical Study of Its Progress from Reimarus to Werde*. Introduction by James M. Robinson. New York: Macmillan, 1968 (First published 1906).

Shanks, Hershel, ed. *Understanding the Dead Sea Scrolls: A Reader from the Biblical Archaeology Review*. New York: Random House, 1992.

Smith, Morton. *The Secret Gospel of Mark*. Cambridge, Mass.: Harvard University Press, 1973.

_____. *Jesus the Magician*. New York: Harper & Row, 1978.

_____. *Clement of Alexandria and a Secret Gospel of Mark*. Cambridge, Mass.: Harvard University Press, 1973.

Spong, John Shelby. *Resurrection: Myth or Reality?* San Francisco: Harper, 1994.

Stauffer, Ethelbert. *Jesus and His Story*. Translated by Richard and Clara Winston. New York: Alfred A. Knopf, 1960.

Sutherland, Stewart R. *God, Jesus and Belief: The Legacy of Theism*. Oxford: Basil Blackwell, 1984.

Tatum, W. Barnes. *In Quest of Jesus: A Guide Book*. Louisville, Ky.: John Knox Press, 1982.

Thiering, Barbara. *Jesus and the Riddle of the Dead Sea Scrolls*. Toronto: Doubleday, 1992.

Trevelyan, G. M. *A Shorter History of England*. Middlesex: Penguin Books, 1959.

Vaage, Leif E. *Galilean Upstarts: Jesus' First Followers According to Q*. Pennsylvania: Trinity International Press, 1994.

Vermes, Geza. *Jesus the Jew: A Historian's Reading of the Gospels*. London: SCM Press, 1983.

_____. *Jesus and the World of Judaism*. Philadelphia: Fortress Press, 1984.

_____. *The Dead Sea Scrolls: Qumran in Perspective*. With Pamela Vernes. Philedelphia: Fortress Press, 1985.

_____. *The Religion of Jesus the Jew*. London: SCM Press, 1993.

Wilkins, Michael J., and J. P. Moreland, eds. *Jesus Under Fire*. Grand Rapids, Mich.: Zondervan, 1995.

Wrede, William. *The Messianic Secret*. Trans. J. C. D. Greig. Greenwood, S.C.: Attic Press, 1971.

Wright, N. Thomas. "The Historical Jesus." *Anchor Dictionary of the Bible*. 6 vols. New York: Doubleday, 1992.

Yancey, Philip. *The Jesus I Never Knew*. Grand Rapids, Mich.: Zondervan, 1995.